Resource Therapy

Primer

Names used in therapeutic examples in this book
are not the
names of actual patients.

Gordon Emmerson, PhD

Copyright Gordon Emmerson 2014
Old Golden Point Press
Blackwood, Victoria: Australia
ISBN-10: 099249950X
ISBN-13: 978-0-9924995-0-1

This publication provides an overview of Resource Therapy. For a more detailed description of the therapy, for numerous illustrations, case examples and transcripts please refer to the main text, *Resource Therapy* (Emmerson, 2014).

"It is only when a person feels emotionally distressed that he or she will decide to seek therapy. Therapy is about helping patients feel better. Patients may be upset about the feelings they are having, upset about the behaviors they are doing, upset about inner conflict, or about their performance. The bottom line is, patients come to therapy because they are upset, not because of how they think."

"The intellect is a barren wasteland in terms of emotion. It is good to have a computer on our desktop or in our head, but it is not a computer that defines us. We connect with others and with ourselves emotionally. We like our friends to be open with their feelings, and we feel understood when others show that they hear our feelings. When we reflect about a sunset, about what we like, or about how we are doing, we are reflecting emotionally. It is our emotions that define us to others and to ourselves. It is emotions that bring patients to therapy, and it is emotions that need to be heard by therapists."

"The best therapists will allow their point of focus to be inside the patient. Everything else about self, the room, anything outside the room, needs to be left behind. The singular focus needs to be inside the story of the patient. It is when that focus stays with the patient that creative therapy follows."

This book is dedicated to my amazing sons, Daniel and Dylan

Inspiration

Support

Ideas

Love

Overview of Resource Therapy

The personality is composed of parts and those parts are our Resources. When they are in a Normal Condition there is Psychological Health. These parts may be:

- **Normal** (Healthy)
- **Vaded** (Exhibit unwanted emotions)
- **Retro** (Exhibit unwanted behaviors)
- **Conflicted** (Parts are in conflict to the point of anxiety)
- **Dissonant** (The wrong part is holding the Conscious)

Resource Therapy allows therapists to respond directly to the personality part that holds the problem. Many therapies speak with an intellectual, talkative, personality part that is not directly related to the presenting issue. Because Resource Therapy attends directly to the personality part that is pathological it is quick and lasting.

RT techniques allow the therapist to learn criteria to diagnose presented issues, and once diagnosed, specific RT Actions are ascribed to each diagnostic classification. The therapeutic process is clear and the treatment regimens are distinct.

Diagnostic categories and some of their associated issues are listed below.

- **Vaded with Fear:** (Phobias, PTSD, Panic, situational fear),
- **Vaded with Rejection:** (Feeling worthless or unlovable, high need for approval),
- **Vaded with Confusion** (Rumination, guilt, blame),
- **Vaded with Disappointment** (Depression, Despair).
- **Retro Original** (Pouting, Anti-Social Behavior, Rage, Personality Disorders, Passive Aggressive)
- **Retro Avoiding** (Addictions, OCD, Withdrawal, Eating Disorders)
- **Conflicted** (Procrastination, Sleep Disturbance, Chronic Fatigue, Cognitive Dissonance)
- **Dissonant** (Frustration in Coping Ability, Below par performance)

The process of Resource Therapy is straightforward: and is called ACAR, see

Table 1.   The first step is to learn what the patient is ready to change (Aim). The second step is to diagnose the pathological Resource State into a category (Classify). The third step is to follow the prescribed RT Actions to help the pathological state to move to a Normal Condition (Actions). The final step is to debrief and review with the patient (Review).

Table 1: The Resource Therapy Process (ACAR)

RT Process	
Aim	Determine what the patient is ready to change.
Classify	Diagnose the Pathological Resource State into a category.
Actions	Follow the prescribed RT Actions for the Classification.
Review	Debrief with the patient.

Resource Therapists learn RT Treatment Actions, or therapeutic techniques. Prescribed combinations of these are used to move pathological Resource States to normality.

Contents

List of Tables

Chapter 1: What is Resource Therapy

Resource Therapy is a psychodynamic therapy that is based on the assumption that personality is composed of parts. In Resource Therapy personality parts are termed Resources. We each have many Resources. When they are non-pathological our different Resources are very useful. We have assertive resources that can help us with difficult situations and difficult people, we have fragile resources that can appreciate the taste of a piece of chocolate, and we have intellectual resources that can consider an idea. The purpose of Resource Therapy is to move pathological resources to a normal condition.

Resource Therapy is based on 5 Assumptions:

1. The personality is composed of parts.
2. Patients react differently from different personality parts.
3. Parts can be healthy or pathological.
4. Pathological parts can be brought back to normality.
5. Pathological parts can be:
   - Vaded   (These parts hold unwanted Emotions.)
   - Retro   (These parts do unwanted Behaviors.)
   - Conflicted   (These parts are in Conflict with each other.)
   - Dissonant   (These parts are Conscious at the wrong time.)

The concepts and techniques of Resource Therapy have been established over the past few years. Table 2 below (Emmerson, 2014) documents when the theories and techniques of Resource Therapy were developed. They represent an extension of the work of Federn (1953), Weiss (1950), and Watkins and Watkins (1997). While Federn and Weiss did not focus on hypnosis in their work, Watkins and Watkins combined the use of hypnosis with Ego State Therapy. Emmerson showed how his techniques of working with personality parts could be used without hypnotic inductions in

Advanced Skills and Interventions in Therapeutic Counseling, 2006. Resource Therapy is based on the work of Emmerson and does not require the use of hypnotic inductions.

Table 2: Theoretical and Technique Developments for Resource Therapy by Gordon Emmerson

Personality Theory based on Personality Parts being physiological neural growth, formed by the repetition of coping skills.			2007
The Concept of Surface and Underlying States, and State Specific Introjects			2003
State Conditions: Normal, Retro, Vaded, Conflicted (coined the term Vaded)			2007
Other aspects of state conditions	Vaded with Fear Vaded with Rejection Vaded with Confusion Vaded with Disappointment	Vaded Conscious Vaded Avoided Retro Original Retro Avoiding Dissonant States	2013
Criteria for Diagnosis into state condition pathological category, and the concept of Sensory Experience Memory			2014
Therapy Process: ACAR – Aim, Classify, Actions, Review			2014
Specific intervention techniques including: Depression, OCD, Addictions, Couples Counselling, Eating Disorders, Crisis Intervention, Grief, DID, Rage, Anti-Social Behavior			2002-2014
Bridging process of Vivify Specific, Attain Age, Funnel			2007
Designated Detailed Therapeutic Actions, including:	Vivify Specific Expression, Introject Speak Removal, Relief Retro State Negotiation	Find Resource Resistance Alliancing Separation Sieve Conflicted State Negotiation	2004-2014

Resource Therapy techniques are called Actions. RT Actions are Core to Resource Therapy. There are 12 RT Actions, plus 3 additional complementary Actions. The complementary Actions are less frequently needed, but are excellent tools when the need arises. For example, RT Action 13 is Resistance Alliancing. This is an Action that helps the therapist view resistance as protection, and describes techniques to ally with the resistant Resource State so therapy can continue. RT Action 1 is Diagnosis. RT Action 2 is Vivify Specific, the technique to make sure the desired Resource is in the Conscious. No one presenting issue will require all RT Actions to be used. The precise selection of RT Actions that will be used with any issue is based on the diagnosis, and is defined in the treatment section of this book.

Important Terms

Resource State

A Resource State is a personality part. It may also merely be called a Resource. In childhood, when we return to a coping skill over and over again the brain grows according to the stimulation it has received. The combination of axon and dendrite growth and trained synaptic firings creates a physiological Resource State that becomes a personality part.

Animal studies confirm that activity grows the brain (Levin, 2010; Wilkinson & Frances, 1995; Blakemore, 1987; Wark, Peck, & Carol, 1982; Buisseret, Gary-Bobo, & Imbery, 1982). Particular types of activity grow the brain where it can perform better in relation to the activity that it has experienced (Brych & Fisher, 2011; Muir, Dalhousie, & Mitchell, 1975). This is obvious when we think about practicing a sport and getting better at that sport. A Resource State is merely a personality part that has grown to be able to perform a role that it has learned through repeated practice

We have many Resource States. I estimate that we have approximately 5 to 15 surface Resource States that we use often. The surface states tend to communicate well together and share memories easily. In other words, the Resource State that speaks to a group will most often have a good memory of what happened when the Resource State that participated in a sport was Conscious.

Synaptic connections between Resource States are not always strong. The person who finds that, while driving there is no memory of the last few minutes, has experienced switching from one Resource State to another, and these two states share a low level of synaptic connections. Another example is most of our childhood Resource States do not share strong synaptic connections with our adult Resource States (states that we have used since childhood). Because of a low level of communication between these states, the synaptic connections between them have atrophied over time.

The same dynamic produces multiple personality, DID. Some children who suffer severe and chronic abuse find a coping skill of not thinking about the abuse, after they change states. This causes synaptic connections between the Resource States to atrophy and the normal Resource States become Alters. Afterward, the synaptic connections between Alters are so weak that one cannot recall what another did when it was Conscious.

Conscious

When we are currently experiencing life from a Resource State that Resource State is said to be Conscious. When one Resource State is Conscious some other Resource States may be observing. This is common with surface Resource States. This indicates that the synaptic connections between the Resource States are strong.

Introject

An Introject is an internalized impression held by a Resource State. An Introject may be an impression of a person, an animal, or an inanimate. Most Introjects are positive and are part of our good memories.

Occasionally, an Introject may be internally feared by a Resource State. For example, a childhood Resource State may have had a frightening experience on a playground and may still hold an internal fear of the bully. This underlying fear may prevent the adult from enjoying outdoor gatherings.

Resource States that hold impressions of Introjects that include, fear, rejection, deep disappointment, or confusion, may attain and maintain a varying level of anxiety in relation to these Introjects. When this occurs the Resource State is said to be Vaded. When a Vaded Resource State comes to the Conscious it brings with it the negative feelings it maintains in association to the Introjects it holds. Therefore, Resource Therapy assists Vaded States to become empowered in relation to their Introjects. This does not mean that they change a memory, but it does mean they recognize that an internalized impression has no power.

There are two kinds of fear. There is external fear and internal fear. External fear is our friend. It keeps us from getting too close to the edge of a ravine. It keeps us from going down a dark alleyway that seems dangerous.

Internal fear is not needed. It is fear of Introjects we hold from the past. Introjects are history, and they cannot hurt us. It may be prudent to fear today's person, but not yesterday's memory. Resource Therapy assist patients to bring out Resource States that hold negative impressions of Introjects so the state can become empowered and gain a feeling of safety and support.

Sensory Experience Memory/Intellectual Memory

There are two types of memory and understanding the nature of these is key to understanding how Resource Therapy techniques work.

- A Sensory Experience Memory is one that, when experienced, the person emotionally re-experiences the original event.

- An Intellectual Memory is one that when recalling an occurrence the emotional experience is not relived.

A Sensory Experience Memory is most normally experienced only closer in time to the event. For example, immediately after experiencing something emotional, good or bad, it is common to relive the emotional experience during recall. As time passes, most Sensory Experience Memories are transformed into Intellectual Memories. Sensory Experience Memories may only be experienced in the longer term when the Resource State that had the original experience is holding the Conscious.

How Sensory Experience Memories relate to Pathology

When a Resource State becomes Vaded the Sensory Experience Memory (SEM) is not transformed over time into an Intellectual Memory (IM). The Vaded State maintains the SEM, probably in an attempt to gain a resolution to the anxiety filled experience, and each time that state comes into the Conscious again, even years later, it re-experiences the SEM. This causes the client to feel out of control and emotionally distraught, often without understanding why. It is most normally the case that the unwanted emotions are experienced without a connection to the Intellectual Memory, therefore the client can feel anxiety, fear, or not good enough without understanding why.

Resource Therapy techniques assist the client to transform the unresolved SEM into an intellectual understanding of safety, support, and empowerment. The SEM is experienced by the Vaded State as if the original occurrence is still happening, so that state needs to gain the emotional calmness that it receives from 'Emotionally' understanding that it is now safe and supported. RT Actions are designed precisely to foster this understanding.

How Sensory Experience Memories can be used to Resolve Pathology

Sensory Experience Memories may be used in therapy to:

- **A SEM can help a State Vaded with Rejection understand that it is lovable.**

  During the RT Action 5, Introject Speak, the client is asked to take on the persona of the rejecting person from the past and is asked a series of questions about its ability to share unconditional love. The Introject of a person who was seen as rejecting will show a poor ability to share unconditional love, and that is why it is viewed as rejecting by the client. Next, the client is directed to immediately return to the state Vaded with Rejection. The State Vaded with Rejection brings back with it the immediate SEM, the feelings of the rejecting introject with its incapacity to share unconditional love. It becomes clear to the client not feeling loved was not because of being unlovable, it was because the rejecting introject was not good at sharing unconditional love. Using a SEM in this way provides a positive enlightenment to the client.

- **A SEM can help** a Resource State Vaded with Confusion gain an understanding about the dynamic of a relationship. This improved understanding can stop the unwanted rumination.

  When Resource States are Vaded with Confusion there is an inability to gain an understanding about the dynamic of a relationship. There is an inability to let something go. The client has an inability to understand how someone my think or feel. By using RT Action 9, the Changing Chairs Introject Action, the client can sit in the chair of the Introject involved in the confusion, then upon returning to the client's chair, the SEM fosters a better clarity and enables the client to feel less confused.

16

- **A SEM can help** a Resource State that has Retro Behavior decide it can be appreciated by taking on new non-Retro behavior.

Retro States behave in a manner that other states do not like. When speaking directly with a Retro State it will often say it will not change, cannot change, or it could never be liked by other states no matter what it might do. The Retro state does not have an experienced of being liked and appreciated by other states and believes it could never be. The following sequence can help a Retro State want to change unwanted behavior to desired behavior.

1. Decide on a new behavior where the purpose of the state can be achieved in a manner that all other states will appreciate.

2. Speak with the state that brought the client to therapy and make sure that state approves the new behavior and speak directly to the Retro state saying it will like that state if it takes on the new behavior.

3. Speak again to the Retro State, and at this time it will be willing to change its behavior because it will hold the immediate SEM of being liked by the other state. This proof of being appreciated is very compelling to a state that has not been liked, so it becomes willing to take on the positive behavior, thus becoming non-Retro, as it no longer carries out behavior that other states do not like.

Chapter 2: Resource Conditions: Normal and Pathological

Normal Condition

We want all of our Resource States to be in a Normal Condition. This is the condition that is not pathological. Resources in a Normal Condition are liked and appreciated by other internal states, and they operate externally in a way that we appreciate. A person with all states in a Normal Condition is psychologically healthy.

Other than Resource States in a Normal Condition there are four general pathological conditions, and eight specific pathological conditions. The purpose of Resource Therapy is to move Resource States from a pathological condition to a Normal Condition.

Resource States that are Vaded or Retro have characteristics that are defined below. The following sections will detail characteristics of the eight pathological Resource States.

Vaded: Unwanted Emotions

Resource States in a Vaded Condition were in a Normal Condition prior to becoming Vaded during an initial sensitizing event(Mackey, 2009; Opperman, 2007; de Graaf, & van der Molen, 1996; Ritzman, 1992; Boswell, 1987). They may have been Vaded with Fear, Rejection, disappointment, or Confusion. They can be problematic for the patient in one of two ways:

> **Vaded Conscious:** These states come into the conscious and exhibit their unresolved emotions in the forms of anxiety, panic, withdrawal.

> **Vaded Avoided:** These states come into or near the conscious and then are immediately driven from the conscious by a Retro Avoiding

State. Vaded Avoided States are the underlying cause of psychological addictions, OCD, and eating disorders.

Retro: Unwanted Behaviors

The one thing in common that all Retro States share is the demonstration of behavior that other Resource States do not like. They may be Retro Original States and demonstrate behavior such as, antisocial behavior, pouting, passive aggressive behavior, and personality disorder behavior. They may also be Retro Avoiding States and demonstrate behavior such as addictions, OCD, and eating disorders.

Because the process of Resource Therapy is to move all states to normality each of the following sections have a table that highlights the condition of the pathology and the condition that it will have when it returns to normality.

States Vaded with Fear

A patient example of the State Vaded with Fear will illustrate how this occurs. A patient, Jane, presented with panic attacks. She said during her panic attacks she felt like she had to get away, or she might die. She said she felt like she needed to pull something away from her throat so she could breathe. And, she said she saw a color she described as 'blue but black'. She did not know why she had panic attacks, and she did not know why she felt the way she did when they occurred.

Bridging (RT Action 3) placed Jane back into her memory of the initial sensitizing event. She was 10 years old, swimming in the ocean, caught in an ocean riptide with her little cousin hanging onto her neck keeping her from being able to breathe properly. Her head would dip into the water and she would see the color 'blue but black'. She thought that she would die if she could not get out.

It is obvious that the emotions Jane's Resource State that was Vaded with Fear felt during panic attacks were a direct reflection of her experience during the initial sensitizing event. Jane's 10-year-old Resource State continued to carry the feeling that its life was in danger. It continued to carry the feeling of panic, therefore when this state came into the conscious Jane would experience panic.

As long as Jane's 10-year-old Resource State carried that feeling of panic it would be able to interfere in her current life. It would do no good to focus on the times when Jane had panic attacks, because they were just a symptom of the fearful emotions held by Jane's 10-year-old state.

RT Actions allow the therapist to diagnose Resource States Vaded with fear and to bring resolution to those states so they no longer hold that fear. Resource States Vaded with fear can cause the following pathologies, among others.

Resources Vaded with Fear can cause these Pathologies

- Nightmares and sleep terror
- Specific Phobia
- Panic attack
- PTSD
- Agoraphobia
- Self-harming behavior
- Generalized Anxiety Disorder
- Dissociative Identity Disorders
- Pathological Gambling
- Addictions
- Workaholism
- OCD (or may be Vaded with Rejection)
- Social Phobia (or may be Vaded with Rejection)
- Business Phobia (or may be Vaded with Rejection)
- Compulsive Shopping (or more often is Vaded with Rejection)
- Antisocial (or may be Retro or Vaded with Rejection)
- Crisis reaction (benefitting from crisis intervention)

The Resource Vaded with Fear	The Normal State
A Resource Vaded with Fear feels there is something that has more power than it does that can hurt it. It prevents the patient from living freely.	Normal States enjoy being in the Conscious. They focus on what is around them, not on a negative feeling.

Resource States Vaded with Fear carry the illusion that the past is still happening. They are still afraid of something from the past. Therefore, the therapeutic interventions for these states make it clear to them that they are now safe, and that the past is not happening. Once these states feel safe and supported, once they are no longer the harbingers of fear, then they no longer interfere in the current life of the patient.

Prior to the initial sensitizing event these states were in a normal condition, and they each had a role, a skill that they offered the personality. While traumatized with fear these states are not able to conduct their original purpose. Following resolution they will again be able to conduct their original purpose, therefore, patients will often describe a re-engagement with activities such as lighthearted play, or nurturance.

States Vaded with Rejection

The most common issue I notice with patients presenting for therapy is Resource States Vaded with Rejection. A patient having a Resource State Vaded with Rejection will report things like:

- I only feel good about myself when I please others
- If I disappoint someone else I feel terrible
- I feel like a fake
- I feel like if other people really knew me they would not like me
- I'm afraid to start the job because I might not be good enough
- I feel unlovable
- I have to fight to get approval

The Resource Vaded with Rejection	The Normal State
A Resource Vaded with Rejection feels it is unlovable, or not good enough. It can keep the patient from engaging, and can cause the patient to question personal value.	Normal States have positive feelings about themselves. They enjoy the time they have in the Conscious and feel they have something to offer.

The underlying common feature of Resource States Vaded with Rejection is a feeling of not being good enough, or not being lovable. These states are the cause of, or are central to, the following pathologies:

Resources Vaded with Rejection can cause these Pathologies
- Social Phobia (or may be Vaded with Fear)

22

- Business Phobia (or may be Vaded with Fear)
- Narcissism
- Anorexia Nervosa
- Bulimia Nervosa
- Antisocial (or may be Vaded with Fear)
- Feeling Unlovable
- Business Phobia (or may be Vaded with Fear)
- Compulsive Shopping (or may be Vaded with Fear)
- Over-competiveness

Resource States Vaded with Rejection have had an experience where they have interpreted themselves as being unworthy, incapable, or unlovable. The truth is all children deserve unconditional love. Resource States that feel unlovable have received that feeling from their interpretation of the Introject of another person. They have felt unloved, or unappreciated by their internal impression of someone else. Therefore, an important aspect of the treatment for Resources Vaded with Rejection is for the states to learn that all children deserve unconditional love, and if they did not receive what all children deserve, that is not the fault of the child.

Of course, this is something that cannot be intellectually transmitted. It is important for the Resource State Vaded with Rejection to return to the initial sensitizing event, then to speak as the rejecting Introject so an emotional understanding can be obtained. That emotional understanding is that at that point in time the Introject was not good at showing unconditional love. This does not mean that the Introject was bad, but it does shift the understanding from, 'I am unlovable', to 'The other person was not able to show me the love that all children deserve'.

States Vaded with Disappointment

Resource States Vaded with Disappointment are upset that life is not how it was planned, or how it was preferred. These states are so upset that they block other states from participating in life in a positive way.

One example is the person who discovered their partner was having an affair. A Resource State can be so disappointed that it will block any other states from enjoying the relationship.

Another example is the person who was fired from a long time job. This Resource State may be so disappointed that it will not allow any other resources to enjoy living. This can, over time, cause psychological depression.

Resources Vaded with Disappointment can cause these Pathologies

- Depression
- Relationship blame
- Prolonged and intense feelings of loss

The Resource Vaded with Disappointment	The Normal State
A Resource Vaded with Disappointment feels low energy, upset, and unwilling for other parts of the personality to be happy.	Normal States enjoy the time they are out and they are thankful for the other states that can help out in various ways. They celebrate the happiness of other states.

It is imperative to understand that it is the interpretation of the disappointment that is important, not actually what happened. Two individuals can experience the same event and one can become depressed, without the other being significantly bothered. The loss of a pet to one person may be an annoyance or even a relief, while to another person it may be devastating.

Therefore, the therapist should always show empathetic understanding to the Resource State that is Vaded with Disappointment. It is only when this Resource State feels understood that it will be cooperative during the therapeutic process.

States Vaded with Confusion

A Resource State Vaded with Confusion ruminates. This is when the patient cannot let a thought go. It keeps returning. This can be confusion about, among other things, why someone committed suicide, how someone felt at the time of their death, what happened to an adopted child, guilt, shame, blame, the actions of another, or the actions of self.

The patient with a Resource State Vaded with Confusion will often have difficulty sleeping. When they attempt to go to sleep the confused Resource State will often take over the conscious and delay sleep.

Resources Vaded with Confusion can cause these Pathologies

- Complicated Bereavement
- Rumination (over the welfare of others, death, or an event)
- Guilt or Shame
- Existential angst
- Deep confusion over the breakdown of a relationship

The Resource Vaded with Confusion	The Normal State
A Resource Vaded with Confusion cannot let something go. There is a rumination about confusion, blame, guilt or shame. Often there is an inability to sleep.	Normal States can let the past be past. They have an ability to experience the present. They have a backward peace and a forward vision.

There is a difference between being confused about the breakdown of a relationship, and being depressed about the breakdown of a relationship. The Resource State Vaded with Disappointment, the depressed state, will experience low levels of energy, and will block other states from enjoying aspects of living.

The State Vaded with Confusion may be able to have energy at work, and other places. It will not block other Resource States from enjoying things. A person with a State Vaded with Confusion may do well during certain parts of the day, but will ruminate when the confused state is conscious.

Retro Original States

Resource States are formed primarily during childhood when coping skills were practiced. A coping skill returned to over and over again that works for the person will become a Resource State. Sometimes the Resource State develops a coping skill that later becomes disliked by other personality parts. This is called a Retro State, a state that carries out activity that is not appreciated by other personality parts. When the original coping skill that formed a Resource State becomes disliked by other personality parts this is termed a Retro Original State. Examples of the Retro Original State may be pouting, withdrawal, rage, and other antisocial behavior.

It is possible for a person to exhibit this behavior and feel quite pleased with the behavior by all personality parts. When this occurs the Resource

State is not retro. A Resource State only becomes retro when its behavior becomes disliked by other personality parts.

Retro Original States can cause these Pathologies
- Anti-Social Behavior
- Withdrawal
- Pouting
- Rage
- Personality Disorders
- Passive Aggressive Behavior

Retro Original Resource States	The Normal State
Retro Original Resource States feel they have an important role to play. They do what they know, and they really do not care if other states do not like what they do.	Normal States carry out behaviors that they feel is important and that other states appreciate also.

The behavior of Retro Original States is behavior that has been conducted by the patient for as long as the patient can remember. It is sometimes the case that a therapist can see behavior that the therapist would like changed, but unless this behavior is recognized by personality parts of the patient as being unwanted, there is little value in focusing on changing that behavior.

Retro Avoiding States

Retro Avoiding States normally take on their avoiding behavior in adulthood. They learn that by conducting a certain behavior the personality is spared the feelings of a Resource State that has been Vaded with Fear or Rejection. For example, the person who checks locks and taps most nights before going to bed may maintain a focus on that activity and proceed through it generally without thinking about anything else. The normal Resource State that does this activity may find that while going through that process the personality is safe from other unresolved emotions. Because this activity serves the purpose of protecting the person from unwanted emotions it may be returned to more often. When the person loses an ability to stop returning to this activity it has become a Retro Avoiding Behavior.

Retro Avoiding Behavior includes all psychological addictions and any other behavior that is not able to be controlled by the patient. The Retro Avoiding State has a purpose to protect the personality from the unwanted feelings of fear or rejection.

Retro Avoiding States can cause these Pathologies
- Addictions
- OCD
- Self-harming behavior
- Obsessive behavior (shopping, eating, work)
- Drug Taking
- Anger or Rage as a means to act out
- Eating Disorders
- Work/relationship avoidance
- Shopping Addiction
- 'Perfectionistic' behavior
- Self-Harming behavior

The State That Comes to Therapy
The State that initially presents to the therapist is not the Retro Avoiding State. The patient with a Retro Avoiding State will almost always report to the therapist that a lack of control is the problem (i.e., drug taking, OCD, addictions, shopping, eating disorders, etc.). The Resource State that originally presents in therapy feels a lack of control. There is behavior that this reporting state does not like and that it cannot stop, therefore it sees this behavior as out of control.

The Retro Avoiding State
The actual Retro Avoiding State feels very much in control while it holds the Conscious. Let's look at an example. Mandy comes home from work to an empty house and begins to feel alone and frightened. These are the feelings of a Vaded State. A Retro Avoiding State has learned how to help Mandy avoid these feelings. It takes over the Conscious, goes to the fridge and eats for the next 45 minutes, holding the Conscious firmly by causing Mandy to feel somewhat 'zoned out'. Other states are blocked during this time, and may even be surprised at Mandy's behavior when they return to the Conscious.

The Retro Avoiding State has become very good at making the personality feel safe during its behavior, in order to avoid the negative feelings of the Vaded State. The Retro State is very much in control, and it feels very useful.

Retro Avoiding Resource States	The Normal State
Retro Avoiding States feel they have an important role to play. They are happy to do what other states do not like if it saves the personality from having negative feelings.	Normal States carry out behavior that they feel is important and that other states appreciate also. They are at peace with other states, and will alter their behavior to bring it in line with the values of other personality parts.

It is almost impossible to cease Retro Avoiding Behavior without first attending to the upset feelings of the Vaded State that is being avoided. It is of little value to work with the Retro Avoiding State until after the Vaded State has returned to normality.

The process of helping the Retro Avoiding State cease its unwanted behavior is to first use imagery to assist the patient to bring into the Conscious the associated Vaded State (see Retro Avoiding, page 73), and second, to work directly with the Retro Avoiding State to ensure that if it is needed again in the future that it can help with a behavior that is seen as positive.

The Conflicted State

Conflicted States are in conflict over a decision or over activities. Imagine coming home from work and thinking about some extra work you need to get done during the evening. Then you find yourself watching TV, feeling a bit guilty, and hearing a little voice in your head saying you are lazy. You ignore the voice and continue watching TV. This is an example of Conflicted States.

Both states are good, the body needs time out to rest and recover, and we need to get work done. The problem is that these two states may not understand the value of each other. The work state may see the rest state as lazy, and the rest state may see the work state as a slave driver.

Another example of Conflicted States are the two states that cannot agree over a major decision. One state says this relationship is not good for me. I deserve better. This is not the kind of relationship I want to have as I grow older. Another state says commitment is important. Family stability is important. There are bad years in a good relationship. Let's just give this more time. Here, these two states are conflicted and again need to learn both to value the contribution of the other, and learn to better communicate so major decisions can be made with less conflict.

Conflicted States can cause these Pathologies
- Procrastination
- Sleep Disturbance
- Chronic Fatigue
- Cognitive Dissonance

Conflicted Resource States	The Normal State
Conflicted Resource States do not understand the importance of other states. They either fight with them to be Conscious, or fight with them to win a decision.	Normal States respect other states and consider what they have to say. They work in a way to compromise with time so all states get the time they need.

We want our states to have different opinions on things and we want them to have different skills. Their diversity enables us to be multi-skilled. We do not want our states to fail to see the value of each other, to fight over which will hold the Conscious, or to discount the values or opinions of other states. Resource Therapy uses Conflicted State Negotiation to assist states to value and honor each other, and to learn to compromise in an ongoing manner.

Dissonant States

Dissonant States do not like being out during the times when they are dissonant. They don't want to be there. They are not the best state to handle the situation.

Dissonant States respond very differently than Vaded States. Vaded States are tender parts of the psyche. They hold unresolved emotion. When they come to the Conscious they bring emotion from the past, emotion that does not match the current situation. Dissonant States do not hold unresolved emotion from the past. They would be normal states if they were not out at the wrong time. They understand they are not doing well in the moment, but they feel like they can't escape the moment.

Examples of Dissonant States include attempting to play a sport and feeling unable to perform as well as you normally would, or taking an exam and not remembering things that were learned.

Dissonant States can cause these Pathologies
- Frustration in coping ability
- Feelings of ineptitude
- Inability to be real self
- Writers block
- Sporting slumps
- Below par performance

Dissonant States should not be confused with Vaded States. Patients who relate higher levels of emotion when describing difficult situations most likely have Vaded States. Patients with Vaded States will not be able to merely find a more preferred state to bring into the Conscious, because the emotions of Vaded States can be very powerful. If a Vaded State is evident, it should be resolved using RT Actions 2 to 7.

Dissonant Resource States	The Normal State
Dissonant Resource States do not feel comfortable when Conscious. They do not like what they have to do when they are in the Conscious, and are frustrated with their ability.	Normal States enjoy their time out. When Conscious, they feel they are the best personality part for that moment. They may want to improve, but they feel able to do that.

The Dissonant State will be happy to allow another state to take the Conscious, once a better state is found to do that. The process of helping a Dissonant State return to normality (that is, come into the conscious only when it is the best state for the time) is to assist the patient to define exactly the preferred manner to handle the situation, and then to find their best

Resource that can do that. A final step is often to use Anchoring (RT Action 15) to make sure the patient will be able to bring the preferred state to the conscious when desired.

Chapter 3: RT Actions and Regimens

Starting and Ending Sessions

The most central objective of the start of a session is to determine what the patient is ready to change. When therapy is ready to begin, I ask the simple question, "What is it that you are ready to change today?" The answer to this question gives is a clear indication for the best direction of therapy. Of course, the focus can change if a larger issue presents itself during the session. It is always important to work on what the patient is ready to change, rather than what the therapist thinks the patient should change.

On following sessions I like to ask, "Since our last session what have you noticed that you are ready to change?" This ensures that session time is not being used on issues that have already been addressed.

The most important aspects at the end of a session is to debrief and review, answer any questions, and end the session with a confidence that the patient will be able to have a more positive experience. Sometimes a patient will ask, "Will I notice much change?" Of course, we can never know exactly how much change a patient will experience, therefore I like to answer questions such as this with, "I don't know. Sometimes it's just nice to be surprised." This type of response does not set up a measurement in terms of what will be expected, but it does leave a positive connotation about the possibilities for the patient to experience change.

During Sessions

During the session it is always good to get a name for the Resource State that you are working with. Make sure that you get this name from the state, itself. A Resource State may not be happy with the name that a different state gives it. When I get a name for a state I circle it in my notes so I can easily refer back to it.

It is imperative to get and use names for Resource States. When you call a Resource State by name it is better able to stay in the Conscious. You can also use the name of a Resource State to call it back into the Conscious after speaking with a different state.

Always speak to, and about, Resource States positively. All Resource States like to be spoken to, and about, with respect and when they are, they are much more cooperative during therapy. Even a Retro State that carries out behavior that should not be encouraged can be referred to as a strong part of the personality. It is good to have strong personality parts, and when they want to cooperate they can be very useful to the patient.

RT Action 1, Diagnosis of Resource Pathology

The goal of RT Diagnosis is to classify the presented issue into one of eight categories, see Table 3, Table 4, Table 5, and Table 6. Almost all patients present with some sort of anxiety.

Table 3: RT Classification Flowchart

1. What is the presenting concern?	2. The Resource might be:	3. When Conscious it feels	4. Has been noticed since Childhood?	5. Diagnostic Classification
Unwanted Behavior	Retro Original	Feels competent	Yes →	Retro Original
	Retro Avoiding		No →	Retro Avoiding
	Dissonant	Feels incompetent →		Dissonant
Unwanted Emotion (Vaded)	Fear	Fear →		V/ Fear
	Rejection	Not good enough →		V/Rejection
	Disappointment	Low Energy →		V/Disappointment
	Confusion	Ruminates →		V/Confusion
Internal Conflict	Conflicted	In conflict with another state →		Conflicted

Table 4: Pathological Resource States

	Pathology of State	Characterisation
4 Vaded Categories (Unwanted emotions)	Vaded with Fear	When Conscious has anxiety or emotions based on fear.
	Vaded with Rejection	When Conscious has anxiety or emotions based on feeling unlovable or not good enough.
	Vaded with Disappointment	Has low energy and one Resource refuses to allow other Resources enjoyment.
	Vaded with Confusion	Rumination, guilt, or shame.
2 Retro Categories (Unwanted behaviors)	Retro Original	Displays unwanted behavior that has been evident since childhood.
	Retro Avoiding	Displays unwanted addictive or OCD behavior. This avoids the vaded feelings of Fear or Rejection
	Conflicted	Two states want the Conscious at the same time or two states disagree on a major issue.
	Dissonant	The state that is Conscious does not want to be out and another state would be preferred.

Table 5 : How Pathological Resource States feel and how they are reported by other states

Pathology	When Conscious it Feels	Other States report that it...
Vaded with Fear	Anxiety or emotions based on fear.	Other states will wish these states would just go away and stop interfering with emotions that get in their way. They attempt to push the emotions away.
Vaded with Rejection	Unlovable or not good enough.	
Vaded with Disappointment	Disheartened and sad. It has low energy.	Other states are blocked by it. No state can have a good time.
Vaded with Confusion	Unable to let something go. Sometimes it feels guilt or blame.	They can't concentrate, work, or sleep because of the state's rumination.
Retro Original	Good about what they do. 'Stay out of my way.'	Other states feel these states get them in trouble. They don't like what they do and they cannot figure out how to stop them. They see them as out of control.
Retro Avoiding		
Conflicted	They feel like they are in a struggle. Will often report an inability to settle.	Other states are aware of the conflict and are frustrated by problems caused by the conflict.
Dissonant	The state that is out does not want to be out and another state would be preferred.	Other states are frustrated by the lack of competence it displays when Conscious.

Table 6: Pathologies Associated with each Classification Type

Classification	Associated Pathologies		
Vaded with Fear	• Nightmares and sleep terror • Specific Phobia • Panic attack • PTSD • Agoraphobia • Self-harming behavior • Generalized Anxiety Disorder	• Pathological Gambling • Addictions • Workaholism • OCD (or Vaded with Rejection) • Social Phobia (or Vaded with Rejection) • Business Phobia (or Vaded with Rejection)	• Compulsive Shopping (or more often is Vaded with Rejection) • Antisocial (or Retro or Vaded with Rejection) • Crisis reaction • Dissociative Identity Disorders
Vaded with Rejection	• Social Phobia (or Vaded with fear) • Business Phobia (or Vaded with Fear) • Narcissism • Anorexia Nervosa • Bulimia Nervosa	• Antisocial (or Vaded with Fear) • Feeling Unlovable • Business Phobia (or Vaded with Fear) • Compulsive Shopping (or Vaded with Fear) • Over-competeiveness	
Vaded with Confusion	• Complicated Bereavement • Rumination (over the welfare of others, death, or an event)	• Existential angst • Deep confusion over the breakdown of a relationship • Guilt or Shame	
Vaded with Disappointment	• Depression • Relationship blame	• Prolonged and intense feelings of loss	
Retro Original	• Anti-Social Behavior • Withdrawal • Pouting	• Rage • Personality Disorders • Passive Aggressive Behavior	
Retro Avoiding	• Addictions • Self-harming behavior • Obsessive behavior (shopping, eating, work)	• Anger or Rage as a means to act out • Eating Disorders • Work/relationship avoidance • OCD	• Shopping Addiction • 'Perfectionistic' behavior • Drug Taking • Self-Harming behavior
Conflicted States	• Procrastination • Sleep Disturbance	• Chronic Fatigue • Cognitive Dissonance	
Dissonant State	• Frustration in coping ability • Feelings of ineptitude • Inability to be real self	• Writers block • Sporting slumps • Below par performance	

The precise diagnosis may not become completely clear before RT Action 2. For example, if the patient presents with anxiety over taking on a new job, it may not be clear whether this anxiety comes from a State Vaded with Fear or a State Vaded with Rejection. When this state is brought to the conscious using RT Action 2 and is able to express the emotions it is experiencing, it will then become clear if it is afraid, or if it has feelings of not being good enough.

Table 7: Recommended Treatment for each Classification Type

Classification	RT Recommended Treatment Actions		
Vaded with Fear	Action 2: Vivify Specific Action 3: Bridging Action 4: Expression	Action 6: Removal Action 7: Relief	Action 8: Find Resource Action 12: Imagery Check
Vaded with Rejection	Action 2: Vivify Specific Action 3: Bridging Action 4: Expression	Action 5: Introject Speak Action 6: Removal Action 7: Relief	Action 8: Find Resource Action 12: Imagery Check
Vaded with Confusion	Action 2: Vivify Specific	Action 9: Changing Chairs Introject Action	Action 12: Imagery Check
Vaded with Disappointment	Action 8: Find Resource	Action 8: Find Resource (Yes, you do this twice)	Action 10: Retro State Negotiation
Retro Original	Action 2: Vivify Specific Action 8: Find Resource	Action 10: Retro State Negotiation	Action 12: Imagery Check
Retro Avoiding	Action 2: Vivify Specific Action 3: Bridging Action 4: Expression	Action 5: Introject Speak Action 6: Removal Action 7: Relief	Action 10: Retro State Negotiation Action 12: Imagery Check
Conflicted States	Action 2: Vivify Specific	Action 11: Conflicted State Negotiation	Action 12: Imagery Check
Dissonant State	Action 2: Vivify Specific	Action 8: Find Resource	Action 12: Imagery Check

RT Action 2, Vivify Specific

The Vivify Specific Action is one of the most used Actions in Resource Therapy. Resource Therapy is powerful because the Resource State that has a problem is worked with directly. The Vivify Specific Action is the Action that ensures that the right state is out for therapeutic work.

Vivify Specific Steps

1. Find one single, specific time the desired state was in the Conscious. This cannot be a general time, such as, "Often with my wife."

2. Ask the Client to allow his or her eyes to close.

3. Begin speaking in the present tense and ask a number of questions to vivify a continuing number of aspects about being in this event, e.g., "As she is looking at you right now, what expression is on her face?"

4. Continue vivifying until you notice that the state you want to speak with is obviously in the Conscious.

5. Ask this Conscious State, "What can I call you, right now, as you are having this experience?"

To bring the right state out it is **IMPERATIVE** to ensure that the patient describes **ONE SPECIFIC TIME** when that state was experienced. It is incumbent upon the therapist to not accept a statement that signifies a general time that state might be out, such as, "When I am at home." The patient must describe one specific incident when the state was out.

When the patient is able to describe one specific incident when the state was conscious the therapist should ask the patient to, "Just allow your eyes to close so you can focus on this better."

Following the closure of eyes, the therapist should begin speaking in **PRESENT TENSE** terms. For example, "With your boss in front of you right now, what kind of expression does he have on his face?" Using these types of present tense questions, a lot of detail should be gathered about what the patient is experiencing during this incident. The following questions are examples of the kinds of details that may help ensure that the desired Resource State becomes Conscious.

- "As you are sitting there in your office, what time of day is it?"
- "Where is the light coming in from? Is it from a window, or from some other type of lighting?"
- "Exactly how are you feeling, right now, as your boss has that expression?"
- "What is the temperature like where you are?"
- "Are there other people watching?"

These kinds of questions may be asked until it becomes evident that the Resource State is in the Conscious. If you are attempting to bring a Vaded Resource State into the Conscious you will be able to see a level of emotion, or affect, exhibited by the client at this time. If you are attempting to bring a Retro State into the Conscious you will notice that you are talking with a state that feels like it has an important role. If you are bringing a Conflicted State into the Conscious you will notice that it shows a level of frustration, dislike, or disapproval about another state. If you are bringing a Dissonant State into the Conscious you will notice that this state does not like being Conscious in the Vivify Specific moment. It will feel incompetent or uncomfortable.

RT Action 3, Bridging

Sometimes patients will report that they know why they had the emotions they do. I find that when they say this they are often mistaken. Bridging is able to reveal exactly what is connected with the Vaded State that is Vaded with Fear or Rejection.

Bridging is important because it links the unwanted emotions of the Vaded States with Fear or Rejection to the initial sensitizing event when they were originally Vaded. It is only by locating the original sensitizing event that the State Vaded with Fear or Rejection may be resolved. For example, a patient may not be able to speak in front of a group because he has a state that was Vaded as a child when he was yelled at by his father. That precise state is still holding a fear of his father Introject from the time it was Vaded. That state will continue to hold that fear until the initial sensitizing event is revisited and the previously Vaded State becomes empowered. Therefore, it is extremely important for Bridging to take the State Vaded with Fear or Rejection to the initial sensitizing event.

Bridging entails three simple steps:

1. Vivify Specific

2. Attain an age for the state.

3. Funnel the state into the initial sensitizing event.

The first step is covered in RT Action 2.

Step 2 continues immediately after Vivify Specific, while the patient's eyes are still closed. The second step is to get the Vaded State that is currently in the Conscious, following step one, to express how old it feels. This can be a little tricky because often if you ask, "How old do you feel?" the patient will merely report the current age. The actual Vaded State will feel the same age that it was at the time that it became Vaded, during the initial sensitizing event.

If, while the Vaded State is speaking you hear a voice that sounds like the voice of a child you can say something like, "It sounds like I'm hearing the voice of a child right now. About how old would that child be?" If this opportunity does not present itself, I often use the following sequence of questions in order to elicit the age that the Vaded State feels.

- "Where exactly in your body are you experiencing this feeling...?" (describe the feeling that has already been expressed)

- "About how big an area does that cover, the size of a golf ball, a tennis ball, a football?"

- "Are the edges of that area distinct, or do they muffle out?"

- "Inside that area, is there a shade of lightness or darkness?"

- "Inside that area, is there a color?"

- "Is that color, or shade, consistent across the whole area, or is it darker in the middle?"

- "If you are standing inside that area right now, is it thick in there, or thin and easy to move?"

- "If you are just sitting on the edge of that area dangling your feet down into that (for example, thick dark red stuff), is it easy to move your feet back and forth, or difficult."

- "What do your feet feel like as you push them back and forth?"

- "Notice what your feet look like in that stuff and tell me?"

At this point patients will almost always say that their feet look smaller. When they do I asked them, "About what age would those feet be?" This series of questions will most normally provide the age of the state at the time that it was Vaded. Even if it is impossible to get an age Bridging may continue with more general questions about kinds of images that are noticed.

The third and final step of Bridging is to funnel the patient into the image of the initial sensitizing event. In order to funnel the patient into the image of the initial sensitizing event I usually use the following questions.

- "Being (for example, seven) right now and feeling (for example, like no matter what you say you're going to be in trouble), does it feel like you are more inside a building or outside a building?"

- "Does it feel like you are more alone, or does it feel like someone else is there?"

- (If someone else is there) "Who else is there?"

- "What is happening?"

There is no need for the patient to go into detail in terms of what is happening. What is important is that they connect with the initial sensitizing event so that they can become empowered over that event using the following RT Actions.

RT Action 4, Expression

When the Vaded Resource State is able to say absolutely anything within the imagery of the initial sensitizing event, it quickly learns that there is nothing internal that can hurt it. It may at first feel too afraid to express its feelings, but with encouragement and assistance from the therapist it will be able to do so. It learns that no matter what it says, it is safe, and it learns that there is nothing that can hurt it internally.

During the expression phase the therapist may say things like:

- "This isn't really happening right now, so you can say anything you want."

- "We know we are in a therapy room right now, so it is safe to say exactly how you feel."

- "Is it okay if I tell him first?"

- "Let's just shrink him down to 1 inch tall. He's just tiny and has a squeaky little voice. Please don't step on him, because I want you to be able to tell him what you want to say."

Empowering statements such as these make it easier for the state that has been Vaded with Fear or Rejection to express.

RT Action 5, Introject Speak

Introjects are internalized impressions held by our Resource States. Just as an actor can take on the role of a person in a play or a movie, a Resource State can take on the role of an Introject, and speak as that Introject. This can be useful in therapy. The Resource State can gain a Sensory Experience Memory from having had the feelings of the Introject. When it returns to reflect on those feelings the Resource State can gain an 'AHA' understanding about the dynamics of the relationship.

Introject Speak can be done with the patient's eyes closed (when working with States Vaded with Rejection), or when applying RT Action 9, Changing Chairs Introject Action, it may be done with the patient's eyes open. By applying the Introject Speak Action the patient may hear from the Introject of a relative, friend, or even a deceased loved one.

When a Resource State is given the opportunity to speak as an Introject that Resource State is able to gain a deeper understanding of the dynamic between it and the Introject that it holds. For example, a Vaded State with Rejection may be asked to speak as the Introject of the person who it felt rejection from. Upon learning that this Introject was unable to share unconditional love because of its own difficulties a deeper understanding of the dynamic is made possible. Therefore, the state that had previously felt unlovable is able to gain the understanding that it was the Introject that was unable to share unconditional love at that point in time.

The first step in Introject Speak is to have the Resource State to say what it wants to say directly to the Introject. Next, the therapist can make a statement such as, "Right now I want to talk directly with dad. I want you to be like a great actor being dad. Just forget who you are so I can hear directly from dad and how he feels right now. Dad, your son has been very brave and has told you that he does not feel like you really love him. Dad, how does that make you feel, when you hear him say that?"

The purpose of Introject Speak is not to change the Introject, the internalized impression the Resource State has of the other person. The purpose is for the Resource State to gain a better understanding of the dynamic between the Introject and the state. If the Introject of a parent says, "My life is too difficult. I should never have had him," then upon speaking with the State Vaded with Rejection the therapist should say, "Thank you for talking with me, dad. Thank you for being honest with me. Right now I want to talk with (The name of the Vaded State). Gee, I can understand why you feel the way you do. Anyone would feel that way. Right now your dad is not able to share the love that every child deserves. Every child deserves unconditional love. I want to make sure that you get the love that every child deserves."

It is by assuming the identity of the Introject, and then returning to the Resource State that the Resource State is able to gain a deeper understanding, due to its Sensory Experience Memory. The Resource State remembers the feelings it had when it pretended to be the Introject, and this allows it to have a cathartic shift in understanding.

RT Action 6, Removal

Removal is very quick and easy, but is an important step. When working with states that have been Vaded with Fear or Rejection, once they have been empowered during the Expression Action, they will be able to decide if they want to allow the Introject to stay in their inner space. Remember, Introjects are Resource State specific, so if one Resource State tells an Introject it wants its space clear of it, that does not affect other Resources and their relationships with that Introject.

Following the Expression Action for an Introject Vaded with Fear, or following the Introject Speak Action for an Introject Vaded with Rejection, the therapist may say something like:

- "That was very good. Now, do you want (Introject name) to stay in your space, or do you want your space clear? It's up to you."

(If the Resource State says it can stay)

- "That's nice. You can just let it know that."

(If the Resource State says it wants it to leave)

- "Just go ahead and tell it to leave."

It does not matter at all whether the Resource State wants the Introject to remain in its space or wants the Introject to leave its space. What matters is that it understands that it has the choice. Understanding that it has the choice is an additional step that allows it to feel empowered in relation to the Introject.

RT Action 7, Relief

Following the empowering Actions, the final step in the resolution of States Vaded with Fear or Rejection is Relief. Relief is an important Action that leaves the previously Vaded Resource State feeling safe and supported.

This Action requires finding another Resource State that can stay with the previously Vaded State to make sure it feels safe and supported. The best way to find a Resource State that has this ability is to ask the patient, by name, how he or she would support a loved one with the same description of the previously Vaded Resource State. For example:

- "Amy, if you saw a seven year old little girl who you know and care about in her room crying and afraid, Amy, what would you want to do?"

When the patient answers this question you can ask,

- "What can I call this part of you that just responded?"

Then, upon getting a response (such as, 'Helper') you can say,

- "Helper, thank you for talking with me. I would like you to go to Hurt, right there in her room, put your arm around her and let love flow from you into every cell and fiber of her being. You can do this, Helper, and everything else you do. The more you do the more powerful you become. You can do many things all at once. Right

46

now just go to Hurt and let her know that you will always be there for her. Let her know she will never, ever be alone."

Then I will ask,

- "Hurt, how does that feel? (And with 'Hurt's' response) Hurt, it sounds to me like you are not feeling hurt anymore. What would be a better name that describes how you are feeling now? What would you like to be called now? (after the answer, e.g., Loved) That is wonderful name. From now on I will call you, 'Loved'."

At the end of the Relief Action the patient will be experiencing a very different affect than was experienced immediately following Bridging. The Resource State that had been Vaded with Fear or Rejection has been changed to a state in a Normal Condition. It no longer holds negative emotions that can surface and cause the patient anxiety.

RT Action 8, Find Resource

Find Resource is used to locate the best Resource that the patient has for the time or activity. It is a straightforward Action, comprised of only two parts. First, a question is asked to determine how the patient wants to experience this time or activity both internally and externally, and secondly the Vivifying Specific action is used to locate and name a Resource that can be available to the patient. For example, if the patient wants to locate a Resource that could better talk with her teenage son, the first question could be:

- "When you are talking with him how do you want to experience the conversation? How do you want to act externally, and how do you want to feel internally?"

You will need to make sure that you get a response for both parts of this question. Then, ask the patient when she has been able to act this way and feel this way with anyone, at any time in her life. Upon getting a response to that question use the Vivify Specific Action to find and name the helpful Resource State. Then, call that state by name, and ask it if it would be willing to help the patient in the future during the times when it is needed.

When resources are asked to help, if they feel able to help, they are happy to do so. Resources love to be conscious and they love to help. It is more often the case that two resources want to be out at the same time, than no Resource State wants to be out.

What if the patient does not have a Resource State that is needed?

If the patient cannot remember a time when he or she was able to act and feel in the desired manner, it is necessary to find a Resource State that can practice and take on that ability. We are not building a new Resource State, merely finding one that has the ability to take on the needed characteristics. In order to find a state that can take on the needed characteristics, ask the patient to describe what it would be like to be able to act and feel in the desired way. The Resource State that can answer this question will be able to practice, and take on the desired activity. For example: (the patient has not been able to remember ever being assertive)

- "Amy, what would it be like to be assertive in the way you would like to be? Just describe how you would talk, how you would feel, and what that would be like for you."

(while getting a description)

- "What can I call this part that is talking right now? What can I call you, this part that really has a good handle on assertiveness?"

(Let's say the name given was 'Strong')

- "Strong, thank you for talking with me. It sounds to me like you have a really good understanding of assertive behavior. Amy needs an assertive part right now, and it seems like you are the best part to help Amy by taking on this behavior. The more you practice it the better you will get at it. Strong, would you be willing, when Amy needs you, to be her assertive part?"

A fragile part could never be assertive, but it will not be a fragile part that describes what it would be like to be assertive. The part that describes what it would be like to be assertive understands that ability well enough to be able to take it on.

RT Action 9, Changing Chairs Introject Action

The Changing Chairs Introject Action helps Resource States to get a better understanding of the dynamic that exists between them and another person. By experiencing sitting in the chair of the other person and returning to their own chair, patients can have a cathartic experience that can help them resolve confusion, guilt, or blame. Patients bring back to their chair the Sensory Experience Memory of the feelings they had as the Introject.

The eight steps below were adapted from *Resource Therapy* (2014) and a more detailed description of this Action can be found in that book, along with case illustrations.

1. **Vivify Specific:** Make sure the pathological state is Conscious and named, e.g., 'Hurt'.

2. **Determine what needs to be said and/or asked:** Speak directly with the Resource, calling it by name, and find out what it would like to say to the Introject if it had a chance, and what questions it would like to ask.

3. **Create an understanding of the Introject in the other chair:** I.e., "Hurt, just imagine the presence of your brother sitting in the chair opposite you right now. Tell me when you have done this."

4. **Ensure complete expression and questions:** Tell the Resource that since we know the Introject is really not in the other chair now, this is a time that absolutely anything can be said completely and safely, and direct the Resource to express itself fully **directly** to the Introject. If the patient says something like, "I want him to know…" stop him or her and say, "Tell him directly. Say his name then continue with what you want him to know." The Resource can also ask any questions that it may choose or benefit from. The therapist should **encourage complete expression** and should take good notes of everything that is said so later when the Introject is speaking all appropriate cues can be made.

5. **Direct the patient to move to the Introject's chair:** After the Resource has been encouraged to fully express, and to fully question, the patient should be asked to stand, move over to the other chair, and when the patient is in the process of sitting down, the name of the Introject should be called out clearly, e.g.,

   - "Anthony, thank you for being here."When the patient has finished sitting down, the Introject should be asked how it feels about what was just said, e.g.,

- "Anthony, she said a lot of things to you just now. How does that make you feel?" This helps the patient settle into the skin of the Introject.

6. **Speak directly with the Introject:** Ask the Introject questions in relation to the needs of the Resource. Ask things that will enlighten the Resource about the abilities, feelings, and level of peace of the Introject. Look at the notes you have taken and make sure the Introject responds to all the comments and questions posed by the Resource.

7. **Direct the patient back to the original chair:** Call the patient by name (not the name of the Resource), and ask him or her to stand up and move over to the other chair, and as the patient is sitting down speak clearly the name of the Resource in order to re-engage with that personality part, e.g., "Hurt, what Anthony said was interesting. He said…."

8. **Debrief with the Resource:** Ask the Resource its feelings about what it has just heard, and see if it has anything else it wants to say to the Introject. Debrief.

RT Action 10, Retro State Negotiation

Retro States carry out behaviors that other states do not like. There are two types of Retro States, Retro Original and Retro Avoiding. Retro State Negotiation may be carried out immediately with Retro Original States, but prior to using this activity with Retro Avoiding States it is necessary to first resolve the Vaded State that is being avoided (see the treatment regimen for Retro Avoiding States, page 73).

Retro Avoiding States are those that carry out all avoiding behavior, such as addictions, OCD, compulsive shopping, and others. A more detailed description of the steps and a case illustration can be found in *Resource Therapy* (Emmerson, 2014).

1. **Use the Vivify Specific Action** (# 2) to bring the Retro State into the Conscious.

2. **Talk with this state to determine how it has helped the patient in the past** in order to become clear on its purpose. For example, a state exhibiting anti-social behavior may have protected the person from attack, or an alcohol abusing state may have protected the patient from the negative feelings of a Vaded State.

3. **Get a name for the Retro State** that is an indication of its purpose, not its role. For example, don't accept the name Smoker, rather accept a name like Relaxer, or Rebel. Don't accept the name Gambler, rather accept a name like Protector. You can suggest a name once the purpose is clear, and you can ask the state specifically what its purpose is. Allow the Retro State to have input on its name.

4. **Show appreciation for how it has helped in the past**, even if the behavior has been negative. You do not need to praise the behavior, just the efforts to help. Praise the state for having been willing to be disliked by other states so that it could accomplish its important role.

5. **Line up an appropriate resource.** If another Resource is needed to handle the situation that the Retro State has handled in the past, use the Find Resource Action (#9). For example, if assertive behavior is needed rather than rage, anger or withdrawal, you will need to find a resource that can be assertive by using the Find Resource Action. You can do this step even before the Retro State Negotiation starts if you prefer. It is just important to have a state that can become conscious during some of the times when the Retro State had been in the past.

6. Suggest an alternative or smaller role that will allow it to continue to accomplish its purpose, a role that the other Resources can appreciate. At this time do not ask the Retro State if it will take on this new role. Say, "Let's just see what other states will think of you with this new (or less used) role. It is common for Retro States to at first believe they will never be liked, or to believe that what they have done in the past is all they can do. They will say things like, "They will never like me," or, "This is just what I do. I can't do anything else." It is amazing how quickly these attitudes change once they have experienced another state appreciating its new role. You can say things like, "I know it seems like they will never like

51

you, but I bet they will if you take on this new way of helping. Let's just see."

7. **Speak directly with the Resource that has presented the Retro behavior** as an issue. Get a name for it. Suggest to it that it will like the Retro State if it changes, e.g., "You would like Protector if Protector only comes out when the body is in real physical danger, and if an Assertive part handles things at other times. That would be really good to have a strong Protector part if wild dogs were attacking, wouldn't it? Then at other times Assertive could handle things. That would be okay with you, wouldn't it?

8. **Speak again with the Retro State** to ensure it is now willing to take on a new behavior or a reduced role, e.g., "Protector, did you hear that. Other states will like you with your new role. Are you willing to allow Assertive to handle most things while you are there in case the body is ever in real danger?"

RT Action 11, Conflicted State Negotiation

Two Resource States can disagree over which will be out (e.g., a work state or a rest state, a sleep state or a thinking state), or two Resource States can disagree over a major decision. There are ten steps to Conflicted State Negotiation.

1. Begin with two chairs facing each other, with the patient in one of the two chairs.

2. Use the Vivify Specific Action to ensure that one of the states in conflict is in the Conscious.

3. Use the Resource State name received from the Vivify Specific Action, and ask the state how it feels about the state that it is in conflict with.

4. Show understanding for its feelings, but make a case to it how important and useful the other state can be.

5. Ask the patient to stand and switch chairs then speak directly with the other conflicted state, making sure you get a name from it for itself.

6. Call it by name and ask it how it feels about the other state that it has been conflicted with in the other chair. Take notes detailing what it says.

7. Show understanding for its feelings, but make a case to it how important and useful the other state can be.

8. Continue making a case until the conflicted state begins to understand the utility of the other state. When it does, pose a compromise where the two states may each be respected and get something that each wants.

9. Again, have the patient switch chairs and make sure the other state is able to respond in the same way, saying how it understands the other's importance and how it wants to work together with it in the future with a specified plan of compromise.

10. Show appreciation to both states for working together and suggest that in the future as circumstances change they will be able to continue to work together and compromise.

When Resource States disagree over a major decision it is often enlightening, both for the therapist and for the patient, to reflect upon the voice of each state when it is expressing its opinion. Sometimes a state may become emotional, indicating that a Vaded State is present and Bridging needs to occur. Sometimes a state may speak with passion, while the other state may speak with obligation. Reflecting on these kinds of observations can assist the patient to resolve the conflict between the Resource States.

RT Action 12, Imagery Check

The Imagery Check Action is an excellent way to check the efficacy of therapeutic intervention, and to allow the patient to gain practice, and to gain a confidence that the intervention has been effective. RT Action 2 is common to all Resource Therapy interventions. Therefore, the therapist already has imagery, and notes about that imagery pertaining to the issue that the patient was ready to change.

Imagery Check is merely returning to the imagery that was problematic in RT Action 2 in order to see if there has been a change in the patient's experience within that imagery. The same types of questions and techniques that were used in RT Action 2 can be used during Imagery Check in order to assist the patient to return to the original imagery. This normally occurs quite quickly because the patient has already established an experience in achieving the imagery, and because the patient is normally more focused during the later parts of the session.

Complimentary Resource Actions

Each of the 12 RT Actions above are used in at least one intervention relating to the eight pathological classifications. The three complementary RT Actions below can be very useful, but are used only when the need arises. Resistance Alliancing is useful when the patient has a level of resistance that interferes with therapeutic progress. The Separation Sieve is useful to assist the patient to let go of something when the patient is ready to move forward. Anchoring is a useful technique to help the patient bring into the Conscious a Resource State that is wanted.

RT Action 13, Resistance Alliancing

Resistance in therapy is an indication that the therapist is close to an emotional Resource State. This means that therapy has been proceeding well. When a therapist witnesses resistance the therapist is witnessing a protecting Resource State. It is good that we have protecting states. Without them we would feel overexposed and fragile. Protecting states are important and they feel their job is important. If they are fought against they will fight back. Therefore, it is good to show Protecting States respect in order to gain their confidence and to help them feel positive about allowing therapeutic progress.

There are two techniques that work well with protecting states.

When you encounter a protecting state in therapy, pause, and say to that state something like,

"I can see there is a protecting part here now. I want to say to you, protecting part, thank you for protecting. I'm sure you have done this for a long time and it is an important thing to do. I want you to keep protecting. I know you are here to protect the part that I want to talk with. I want to help that part also. Right now while I am here, this might be a good time for you to take a well-deserved rest. You have worked very hard, but I want you to keep an eye open just to make sure everything is okay. Be ready to protect, if you are needed. But in the meantime I really appreciate you letting me continue with the work to help the state that you have protected for so long."

I find this technique works for most resistance. I do not verbally engage with the protecting state by asking it to respond. I merely show respect to it, and for what it does. Sometimes there is an intellectual state that does not respond to this demonstration of respect. Sometimes the client will continue to intellectualize and stay in the head. Therapeutic issues are emotional issues. It is emotions that bring patients to therapy.

The second technique for dealing with resistance is specifically for intellectual states that want to maintain safety by staying in the head. For example,

- "I can see there is a very powerful intellectual part there. I am wanting to talk with a fragile part. I assume you know that it is there, since this person came to therapy because of its feelings. Right now, intellectual part, I will just call you, 'Intellect', if that is okay. Intellect, you are aware that that fragile part is there, aren't you?"

('Intellect' responds affirmatively)

- "What do you think of that fragile part, Intellect? Do you like it? Do you wish it was not there? What do you think of it?"

('Intellect' responds that it is not liked and wishes it would just go away and stop getting in the way.)

- "Thank you for telling me. I just want to see what that fragile part feels about what you just said. Fragile part, Intellect has just said that he does not like you, and he just wishes you would go away. That must not feel very good to you, Fragile part. How do you feel when you hear him say that?"

At this point the fragile part is able to respond, because the intellectual part is interested in hearing the response. The intellectual part is curious, has made a comment about the fragile part, and wants to know what the fragile part will say about its own comment.

Immediately, when the fragile part responds, it is good to thank it for speaking, and get a name for it. Once you have a name for it continue to call it by that name, often, and that will help it stay in the Conscious. When I say often, I mean annoyingly so. Use its name in every sentence.

RT Action 14, The Separation Sieve

The Separation Sieve is a technique that allows a Resource State to separate itself from something it is ready to let go of. For example, a Resource State may be ready to let go of guilt, maybe ready to let go of a past relationship, or maybe ready to let go of a feeling of trauma.

While I prefer the techniques of RT Actions 2 to 7 to resolve trauma, the Separation Sieve may also be used to resolve trauma. It is non-coercive, and does not require an ISE to be revisited.

The Separation Sieve involves a 10 step process. The steps will be listed below followed by a short explanation with each step.

1. Make sure the correct Resource is in the Conscious.
   Unless it is already obvious, use the Vivify Specific RT Action to make sure that the right Resource is in the conscious.
2. Check to see if the patient is ready to let go.
   Speak directly with the Resource about whether or not it is ready to let go. It is good to tell it that the Separation Sieve is merely an experiment, and after it is used it will be able to make up its own mind if it wants everything back the way it was, or if it wants a change.
3. Describe the sieve.
   Tell the patient that it is now okay to allow his or her eyes to close. Describe the sieve as being much more powerful than it needs to be. Tell the patient that he or she will be easily able to come through the sieve but that the sieve cannot possibly let anything heavy through. Any anger, guilt, resentment, negativity, is like a heavy coat that can fall off and be caught in the sieve so that the light part can easily come through, "Down to where my voice is."
4. Describe coming through the sieve leaving everything heavy behind.
   Suggest to the patient that right now he or she is easily falling through the sieve, "Down to my voice, just as an experiment to see what it feels like."
5. Ask the Resource how it is feeling.
   Ask something like, "What does that feel like now, with all that heavy stuff caught in the sieve?"
6. Ask the Resource to look back up into the sieve and describe what that stuff looks like that was left behind.

Say something like, "Look back up into the sieve and symbolically tell me what that stuff in the sieve looks like." (It is normally described as sticky and dark.)

7. Ask the Resource if it wants any of that stuff back.
   Say something like, "Do you want any of that stuff back?"

8. Ask the Resource what color of light, or fluid, would sizzle that stuff completely away.
   Say something like, "What color of light, or fluid, would sizzle that stuff into nothingness?"

9. Provide the image of the stuff in the sieve sizzling away with the light or fluid.
   Say something like, "Okay then, let's just allow that purple light, much more powerful light than it needs to be, to just sizzle that stuff all way. Czzzzzzzzzzzzzzzzzzz" (Yes, I make the sound.)

10. Ask the Resource how it feels now.
    Say something like, "How are you feeling now?"

I may see a number of patients without using the Separation Sieve, but occasionally it is very helpful in assisting the patient to let go of something that has been difficult for them to release. Occasionally, a person will see something in the sieve that he or she is not ready to let go of, and if this is the case they can just allow that part through. An example of this is, a patient may not be ready to let go of every aspect of a past relationship, so they can just let through the aspects of that relationship that they want to continue, and sizzle everything else away.

Obviously, the separation sieve is a metaphor that allows the patient to gain a focus on exactly what is wanted, and what is not wanted. The patient becomes a willing participant in an activity that clearly designates what they want to let go.

RT Action 15, Anchoring

Anchoring is a useful tool to help empower the patient to bring into the Conscious a Resource State that is desired. Patients will be able to bring into the conscious their desired Resource States as long as a Vaded State is not involved. Vaded States often hold overpowering emotions and until resolved they can prevent the patient from being able to bring in the preferred state.

For example, a patient with a Vaded State having a fear of dogs would not be able to easily set that state aside to feel comfortable with dogs.

Three other Actions are used in anchoring.

1. The **Vivify Specific Action** is used to vivify a time when the patient wants to bring in a preferred state.

2. Next, the **Find Resource Action** is used in order to find the preferred state.

   Once the preferred state is found, and named, that state is asked what type of animal it most associates with itself.

   It is asked to describe the animal in some detail, to describe its breathing, to describe the setting that it is in, and to describe what it feels like being this animal. The animal becomes the anchor.

3. Finally, the **Imagery Check Action** is used to allow the patient to practice remembering the feeling of the animal within the image whenever the associated Resource State is desired.

In *Resource Therapy* (Emmerson, 2014), Anchoring is illustrated with the example of a patient wanting to improve sporting performance.

Chapter 4: Treatment Regimens for each Classification

Vaded with Fear

RT Action 2, Vivify Specific

One of the most important aspects of treating a patient who has a State Vaded with Fear is to first make sure that the Vaded State is Conscious. This means that RT Action 2, Vivify Specific, must be used in order to bring out the specific time this Vaded State has been conscious.

If the Vaded State is a Vaded Conscious State this process is not difficult. The patient will present with the issue being the negative emotions that are experienced when this Vaded State is conscious. Therefore, the therapist merely needs to vivify a precise time that the state is conscious using RT Action 2.

If the Vaded State is a Vaded Avoided State the process is a bit more complex. The Vaded State may have only been out for a moment prior to a Retro Avoiding State taking over the Conscious in order to save the personality from the negative feelings of the Vaded State. This means that the therapist needs to use imagery to find the precise time the patient decided to use the Retro Avoiding Behavior. Imagery may be used to assist the patient to imagine delaying the Retro Avoiding Behavior within the imagery. When this is done properly the anxiety of the patient will increase, and this increase in anxiety is the Vaded Avoided State coming into the Conscious. At this point Bridging may occur. Transcribed case examples of this dialog are available in *Resource Therapy* (Emmerson, 2014).

RT Action 3, Bridging

When Bridging to a State Vaded with Fear, it is sometimes the case that the patient will exhibit an emotionally reactive behavior. If the therapist is not willing to work with a patient exhibiting high levels of emotion, Bridging should not be used. It can be re-traumatizing to bridge the patient to a traumatic initial sensitizing event, if no therapeutic intervention follows. It is de-traumatizing to bridge the patient to a traumatic event and then resolve that trauma using the Expression, Removal and Relief Actions.

Some therapists are not comfortable with patients when they show anxiety. These therapists will sometimes attempt to move the patient immediately away from anxiety by relaxing them and giving them positive images to help them feel better. This is precisely the wrong thing to do when working with Vaded States. When the patient is moved away from anxiety the patient is moved away from the state that needs resolution. It is imperative that the state that needs resolution gain the empowerment and support that it needs. It cannot do this unless it is in the Conscious.

Patients with States Vaded with Fear will demonstrate different levels of affect following Bridging. Regardless of the level of affect, it is important for the therapist to move directly to the Expression, Removal, Relief resolution Actions when the initial sensitizing event has been located.

RT Action 4, Expression

When the patient fears the Introject of another person, the Introject of an animal, or the Introject of something like a fire, a flood, or storm, Expression to what has been feared is empowering. The therapist should make it easy for the patient to express to what was in the past feared so the patient will be able to understand there is nothing currently internal that is harmful.

The therapist may make it easy to express by suggesting that the feared Introject be shrunk, moved further away, or the therapist may speak to the feared Introject first. It is important that the Vaded State speak directly to the

Introject it has feared, because this is a step that allows it to understand it can say absolutely anything safely. There is nothing internal that can hurt it.

RT Action 6, Removal

Following Expression, the Resource State is given the opportunity to decide whether it wants its Introject to stay in its inner space or leave. It does not matter how this decision is made. Having the power to make this decision is empowering.

RT Action 7, Relief

An important step in resolving a State Vaded with Fear is to find a nurturing, internal Resource State that can stay with it and give support to the previously Vaded State. As explained in the Actions section of this book, it is important to find a state that wants to do this.

At the end of this, Relief Action, it is good to ask the previously Vaded State if it would like a new name. A state that may have previously been named 'Frightened 'may choose a new name, such as, 'Safe'. It can be asked to choose a name that fits how it feels currently.

RT Action 8, Find Resource

A State Vaded with Fear may have prevented the preferred Resource State from taking on an activity. For example, a State Vaded with Fear may have prevented a communicative state from being able to talk in front of a group. Following the resolution of the State Vaded with Fear it can be helpful to use the Find Resource Action to find the most appropriate state for the activity. For example, a state that enjoys communicating can be found to help the patient enjoy communicating to groups, following the resolution of that Vaded State.

RT Action 12, Imagery Check

The original image from RT Action 2 can be used in the Imagery Check to ensure that the patient no longer experiences the unwanted emotional reaction.

Vaded with Rejection

RT Action 2, Vivify Specific

A State Vaded with Rejection will feel unlovable or incompetent. If a patient presents with this as the issue they are ready to change, use the Vivify Specific Action to ensure that the Resource State with this undesired feeling is in the Conscious.

RT Action 3, Bridging

When Bridging to a State Vaded with Rejection the patient will go to an ISE where a state was unable to feel an unconditional acceptance.

- Sometimes a state feels neglected, or unnoticed by a parent,

- sometimes the ISE will be at a time when one parent is leaving the household following a relationship separation, and

- sometimes the ISE will be at a time when a younger sibling is seen as getting more love.

These states have in common Introjects of a parent or Guardian that has not revealed to them unconditional love. This does not mean that the memory of the patient is accurate, but it does mean that the Vaded State feels to some degree, unlovable.

RT Action 4, Expression

Expression is an important step when there is a Resource State Vaded with Rejection. It is important for the state to be able to say, directly to the protagonist, how that person's action causes it to feel. The patient may be encouraged to say things like, "I need you. Why are you leaving?" If the state indicates that they were spoken to in an inappropriate manner, it may be encouraged to say something like, "You have no right to speak to me like that. The way you are speaking to me is wrong."

Statements such as these empower the Resource State Vaded with Rejection. They enable the Resource State to understand that they have the power to say anything that they want.

RT Action 5, Introject Speak

When a Resource State has been Vaded with Rejection it is important for it to be able to hear directly from the rejecting person. Following Expression, the therapist can say something like,

- "That was very good. Right now, I want to hear directly from Dad. I want you to be like a great actor, forget who you are, so I can hear directly from Dad. You can speak as him now. Dad, your daughter said a lot of things to you right now. How does that make you feel, Dad?"

- If the Vaded State reports being alone, it is for the rejecting person (who SHOULD be there) to speak, not a person the state would like to be there.

Because the Resource State feels rejection from the Introject, the Introject will always respond in a less than unconditionally loving manner. This reflects the internalized impression the Resource State has of the Introject.

The Introject may say things like, "Of course I love her. I work all day because of her." But, when asked to express that love back to the Vaded State

65

the Introject will say things like, "Well, she knows I love her." Introjects will sometimes say things like, "She is very demanding. I have too many things to do. I should not have had kids."

There is no attempt to change an Introject. This would seem inauthentic to the patient. It is okay if a patient has an understanding that a parent was not unconditionally loving. That understanding does not have to be changed. What needs to be changed is the experience of the child feeling unlovable. Therefore, after Introject Speak it is a very important step to return and speak directly with the Vaded State and say something like,

- "I can really understand why you feel the way you do now. Your 'Dad' is not very good at showing unconditional love. Every child deserves unconditional love, no matter what. Even when they make mistakes, every child deserves unconditional love. I want to make sure you get the love that every child deserves."

Statements like these change the experience from, "I am unlovable," to, "I did not receive the love that every child deserves." There is no attempt to make the Introject a villain. Statements can be made like, "I'm sorry at this point in his life your dad was not able to show unconditional love. Hopefully, later he can get better at doing that."

RT Action 6, Removal

The Removal Action is the same as it was for working with Resource States Vaded with Fear. The state is merely asked whether or not it prefers the other person to remain in its inner space. It does not matter how this question is answered. It is the power that it perceives in being able to answer the question that is important. For example,

- "I want to make sure you get the love you deserve, in the meantime do you want your dad in this space where you are right now on the inside, or do you want a clear space? You can have it anyway you want, and it will not affect what your adult parts do."

If the state says, "I don't want him here," or, "He can leave," I just say, "That's fine. Just tell him he can go now." The fact that the previously Vaded State has been able to say absolutely anything and still be okay gives it the power to have its inner space the way it prefers.

If the state says, "No, he can stay," I just say, "That's nice. Just let him know he can stay."

RT Action 7, Relief

This is where a helping Resource State is brought in to assist the previously Vaded State. See RT Action 7, page 46, for instructions. At the conclusion of this Action the patient should feel safe, supported and loved. If a negative sounding name had been given to the Resource State, at this point it is good to ask the state what name would better fit the way it feels now. Patients will sometimes report that when the state was able to change its name to reflect its new feelings the change somehow felt institutionalized.

RT Action 8, Find Resource

Following the resolution of the Vaded State, that state will be in a Normal Condition. States Vaded with Rejection are almost always childhood states, therefore it is unlikely that it will be the best state, the most preferred state, for the patient to handle the situation described in RT Action 2.

RT Action 8, Find Resource (see page 47) can be used to ensure that the patient will have the most preferred Resource in the Conscious for those times in the future.

RT Action 12, Imagery Check

The final Action, once preferred resources have been found to deal with a situation in the future, is to do and Imagery Check in order to allow the patient to experience the imagery of the original presentation with the new and preferred Resource in the Conscious (See RT Action 12, Imagery Check, page 53).

Vaded with Disappointment

States Vaded with Disappointment block other states. They operate like a semitrailer turned crossways on the freeway. They do not let other states enjoy anything. States may be Vaded with Disappointment about one particular issue, or about life in general. A person in a partnered relationship may discover that their partner has had an affair. They may have a state so disappointed that it will block all other states from enjoying the relationship. In this example, only states involved in the relationship may be blocked, as the person may be able to operate almost normally at work and with friends.

Psychological depression occurs when a Resource State becomes so disappointed that it blocks all states from enjoying living. In order to assist a patient to change the blocking behavior of the state Vaded with Disappointment it is important to express to that state in a way that it can feel understood. If it does not feel understood by you then it may not cooperate in therapy.

Another aspect of working with a patient who is depressed is the speed that work can progress. While psychological depression is caused psychosomatically, there is also a physiological component. The body physiologically slows down and it appears to take at least several days for energy to be restored to the body. As energy is restored to the body, work can progress more easily.

A step to helping a patient who has psychological depression is to find two resources that have enjoyed activities in the past, and that are willing to enjoy them again, then to gain permission from the depressed Resource State for them to begin that enjoyment.

The depressed Resource State will allow this to happen, and will cooperate, if it feels understood and appreciated by the therapist.

RT Action 8, Find Resource

The first step in helping a depressed patient regain energy is to find a Resource that has enjoyed an activity in the past. This is not as easy to do as it sounds. Depressed patients will often say they had never enjoyed anything in the past. But, if you ask the patient to search his or her memory and intellectually remember something that was enjoyed, the patient will be able to do this. The only difference in using the Find Resource Action with non depressed patients and using this Action with the depressed patient is the difficulty the patient has in remembering something that was enjoyed in the past.

When the patient is able to remember a specific time that was enjoyed in the past, that time can be vivified until the energy of the patient changes. When the patient shows positive energy of enjoying the activity, a name can be obtained for that Resource State, and it can be asked if it would be willing to enjoy that activity again if it gets permission to do that from the state that is upset.

RT Action 8, Find Resource

The same process described above needs to be completed with a second Resource State that has been able to enjoy something in the past, and that is willing to again enjoy that activity when granted permission.

At the end of the second Find Resource Action you will have two resources that have agreed to reengage with an activity that they have enjoyed in the past (if they are granted permission to do that).

RT Action 10, Retro State Negotiation

The next step is to engage with the depressed Resource State. It is easy to find the state, because it dominates the personality. All you will need to do is ask the patient to describe their recent emotional experience. It will be the depressed Resource State that describes this experience.

It is good to thank this state for speaking with you, show understanding for its level of despair, let it know it has a right to feel upset, and then ask it, even though it is upset if it would be willing for the two states that you just spoke with to reengage and enjoy what they do. You can tell the state that you want to begin working with it, not so things will be like they were in the past, but so it can make a positive contribution in the future.

This is about all that can be done in the first session of working with someone who has a Resource State suffering from Disappointment. The depressed person exhibits an obvious low level of energy. There is nothing that can be done in a single session that will dramatically change this. It takes time for this energy level to increase.

When the patient returns the next week there is normally a marked improvement in energy, although it is often still low. The increased level of energy improves the chances of having a positive outcome when working with the Resource State that is Vaded with Disappointment.

Depending on what caused the state to feel disappointment Retro State Negotiation can be used in a way that will either reduce responsibility of the Vaded State or find a new responsibility for that state. During this work it is important that the therapist continue to show respect that things will not be as they were, while at the same time indicating that the state that had been Vaded with Disappointment is important and it is important that it continue to contribute.

When the state that has been Vaded with Disappointment finds a way to accomplish its purpose through alternative activities, the patient will show marked improvement. Focus should be on the purpose of the state, "What is your role? What is the purpose of what you have done in the past? How have you helped this person in the past?"

When you find the purpose of the state then you can find a new alternative way that state can accomplish that purpose. Again, it is most important not to indicate that things will be as good as they were. It is important to indicate that the state can contribute in a meaningful way.

Often patients will be misdiagnosed with depression. It is not unusual for a patient come to therapy that is suffering from a State Vaded with Fear, Rejection, or Confusion, who has been diagnosed with depression. If it becomes clear that a Resource State has been Vaded with Fear, Rejection, or Confusion, follow the treatment regimens associated with those pathologies.

Vaded with Confusion

Resources Vaded with Confusion ruminate. It will not be able to let something go. The patient often reports not being able to sleep, and will often report thinking about the problematic issue many times during the day.

RT Action 2, Vivify Specific

The first step in helping someone resolve a State Vaded with Confusion is to make sure that state is in the Conscious. In order to do this begin a conversation with the patient specifically about the matter of confusion. This will bring the confused state into the Conscious, and this should be evident by a display of low-level anxiety.

Talk with the state and discover some detail about the confusion. The next step will be for that state to have a conversation with an Introject that is the root of the confusion. This Introject can be a living person, a deceased person, a pet, or even an inanimate.

RT Action 9, Changing Chairs Introject Action

Use RT Action 9, ensuring that the confused state expresses completely to the Introject in the other chair. Make sure you take good notes so that when the patient changes chairs you will be able to speak with the Introject in a way that ensures it responds to the patient, to all the points in your notes.

Upon returning to the chair of the Confused State, that state will remember the feelings it experienced while in the chair of the Introject. There appears to be something about having experienced feelings from the chair of the Introject that resolves confusion held by the Resource State.

RT Action 12, Imagery Check

Use the Imagery Check Action to vivify times when the patient had been confused in the past, for example when trying to sleep, in order to ensure that the cycle of confusion has been broken.

Retro Original

RT Action 2, Vivify Specific

It is quite straightforward to locate the Resource State using the Vivify Specific Action. The patient will have presented complaining about an aspect of their own behavior, such as rage. The Vivify Specific Action can be used to place the patient in the precise moment when the Retro State was Conscious so that it may be spoken with directly.

It is safe to bring out any Retro State because the process of Resource Therapy is one of showing appreciation to the state, and always giving it a choice to change so that other states may appreciate it even more. In other words, we do not get into a conflict with any Resource State. It is very important to consistently praise all Resource States. This is what causes them to want to cooperate, helps them feel good about themselves, and helps them to be ready to change. This does not mean that we praise negative behavior. It does mean that we can praise strength and a desire to help.

RT Action 8, Find Resource

While speaking with the Retro State it often becomes clear that it is not the best state to be out for the situational requirement. If this becomes clear prior to the Retro State Negotiation, RT Action 10, it is good to find the best Resource for the situational requirement. That way, during the Retro State Negotiation this preferred resource can be available to be a part of that negotiation.

In order to find the best Resource, merely use the situational imagery from the Vivify Specific Action, then ask the patient exactly how this situation would best be handled both internally and externally. Use the Find Resource Action to ensure that the appropriate state is chosen.

RT Action 10, Retro State Negotiation

The Retro State Negotiation Action is used exactly as described under the Actions Section of this book to ensure that both

- the Retro Original State has a role that is appropriate for it, that other states appreciate, and that is good for the patient, and

- the preferred Resource that was found to handle the problematic situation is happy to be helpful.

RT Action 12, Imagery Check

The Imagery Check Action is used to bring back the original imagery from RT Action 2 in order to ensure that all states are working positively together.

Retro Avoiding

RT Action 2, Vivify Specific

The Vivify Specific Action needs to be done carefully when working with Retro Avoiding States. Retro Avoiding States believe they have an important role. They are saving the personality from the unwanted emotions of the Vaded State. It does no good to begin work attempting to convince a Retro Avoiding State to change. It may agree to change but when needed again, when the Vaded State emotions come to the surface, most often the Retro Avoiding State will step in to help the patient avoid the negative feelings.

Vivify Specific, when working with a Retro Avoiding State, is at first used not to bring out the Retro Avoiding State, but to bring out the Vaded State that is being avoided. Therefore, it is important to ask the patient to describe precisely the moment immediately prior to Retro Avoiding Behavior. In other words the patient is not asked to describe the Retro Avoiding Behavior, the patient is asked to describe the point immediately prior to the initiation of the Retro Avoiding Behavior. For example, if the Retro Avoiding Behavior is checking locks and taps, the patient might be asked to describe what they feel like, lying in bed, before they get up to check the locks and taps. The patient can be asked to imagine lying in bed a bit longer, in other words to delay the Retro Avoiding Behavior, and this will bring the associated

Vaded State to the surface. When the anxiety of an Avoided Vaded State is evident it is time to Bridge.

This, finding the right state, finding the Vaded State, is the most important aspect of stopping Retro Avoiding Behavior. Unless the associated Vaded State can be brought to the surface for Bridging it is very difficult to stop this behavior. If the associated Vaded State can be brought to the surface, and resolved, there will be no need for the Retro Avoiding Behavior.

RT Actions 3 to 7 should be used identically to how they are used to help any Resource State Vaded with Fear, or Resource State Vaded with Rejection. Refer to the resolutions for States Vaded with Fear or Rejection in Chapter 4, above.

RT Action 3, Bridging
RT Action 4, Expression
RT Action 5, Introject Speak
RT Action 6, Removal
RT Action 7, Relief

Following the resolution of the Vaded State another step needs to occur. Without another step the behavior of the Retro Avoiding State will stop, sometimes permanently, but sometimes it will return. The Retro Avoiding State has used an unwanted behavior to help the patient avoid the feelings of the Vaded State. Unless this Retro Avoiding State gains a new behavior that it can help with in the future, at some future date the patient may become emotionally distressed, therefore the Retro Avoiding State may return to the avoiding behavior in an attempt to help the patient reduce distress.

RT Action 10, Retro State Negotiation

During the Retro State Negotiation make sure that you discover the purpose of the Retro State. It will probably be to assist the patient to have less distress. Negotiate with the Retro State to find another way it can do this in the future if it is needed. By continuing to praise the Retro State, and appreciate the work that it has done in the past, it will be willing to take on a new role.

Sometimes it will not commit to a new role before a different state is asked if it would like the Retro State once a new role is adopted. States like to be liked and when the Retro State hears directly from another state that it will be liked by taking on a new activity, if needed, it will more likely be happy to change.

RT Action 12, Imagery Check

Use Imagery Check as normal to confirm the efficacy of the resolution.

Conflicted States

The process of working with Conflicted States is straightforward. Conflicted States are either two states that both want to be conscious at the same time, or two states that disagree on some major life decision. It is important for the two states to learn to respect and honor each other. They need to learn to have internal communication so that a compromise can be made and can continue to be adjusted.

Conflicted States have, in the past, not respected the value of the other. It is important that the therapist shows support for each state in conflict so each can see the value of the other, compromise, and continue a useful internal dialogue.

The three Actions below should be carried out precisely as they are described in the Actions section of this book.

RT Action 2, Vivify Specific
RT Action 11, Conflicted State Negotiation
RT Action 12, Imagery Check

Dissonant

Dissonant States are otherwise normal states that are conscious at the wrong time. They do not want to be conscious at the wrong time. There may be wonderful roles that they can play, but when they are conscious at the wrong time the patient feels incompetent, in the wrong skin, and unable to handle the situation in a preferred manner.

RT Action 2, Vivify Specific

Is not difficult to use the Vivify Specific Action to locate the Dissonant State. If the patient has presented with this as a concern, the patient will be able to easily tell you a particular time when the Dissonant State has been Conscious.

Upon bringing the Dissonant State to the Conscious and getting a name for it, it may be asked if it would mind if the therapist finds another state that can handle the kinds of situations that it does not feel comfortable handling. The Dissonant State is very pleased for another state to take over duties that it does not like (See *Resource Therapy*[2014] for several illustrations of this, and examples of therapeutic interventions).

RT Action 8, Find Resource

Apply RT Action 8 exactly as it is presented in the Actions section of this book. An additional Action that the therapist might consider using in order to assist the patient to bring out the preferred state is RT Action 15, Anchoring. If it appears that the patient will have no difficulty accessing and bringing out the preferred Resource State there is no need to use the Anchoring Action.

RT Action 12, Imagery Check

Use Imagery Check, as normal, to confirm the efficacy of the Dissonant State resolution.

Chapter 5: Treatment Process for specific Presentations

Addictions: gambling, drugs, workaholism, obsessive compulsive disorder, and others

Everything happens for a reason. When a person habitually does something that they really do not want to do, a reason exists for their behavior. Even though they do not want to do the behavior they are getting something positive from it. The behavior that they return to over and over again is helpful because it allows patients to escape from the negative feelings of Vaded States.

Addictive behavior would make no sense if one were to assume that the personality was not composed of parts. A person would not do something that that person did not want to do. In reality, the personality is composed of parts. The part that carries out addictive behavior is not the same part that complains about that behavior.

Retro Avoiding States are involved in all psychologically addictive behavior. Table 8 is an illustration of the dynamic between Vaded States and Retro Avoiding States. While all Vaded States are not avoided (Vaded Conscious States), some Resources Vaded with Fear or Rejection are driven from the Conscious by Retro Avoiding States.

Table 8: The Vaded State Retro Avoiding State Dynamic

Cue	A State Vaded with Fear or Rejection (Vaded Avoided)	A Retro Avoiding State
A patient lays down to sleep	Begins to feel anxiety	Checks locks and taps (OCD)
A patient has a day off	Vaded State feelings surface	Workaholism
A patient attempts to socialise	Fears of adequacy	Drug Behavior
A patient enters an empty house	Feels lonely or afraid	Eats

The dynamic between Retro States and Vaded States is not difficult to break, but it must be done in the precise chronological order. The Retro State is the Savior of the personality. It saves the personality from the negative feelings of the Vaded State, therefore as long as a Vaded State has negative feelings the Retro State feels it has an important job to do.

It does little good to work directly with the Retro Avoiding State before the negative emotions of the Vaded State have been resolved. For example, it is possible to use the Vivify Specific Action to speak directly with the Resource State that gambles. The state will be aware that other states do not like its activities, and it may even promise to stop gambling. Later, when the negative feelings of the Vaded State surface it is this Retro State that responds. It has a subconscious understanding that its avoidance behavior is more important than being appreciated by other states, and more important than upholding any deal that it has made with the therapist.

Here is the correct chronology for assisting the patient with addictive behavior:

Use the Vivify Specific Action to speak directly with the Retro Avoiding Resource State, and show appreciation to the state for its hard work in protecting the personality. The state will at once be surprised and appreciative of the respect it gets from the therapist. It is accustomed to working hard, and being disliked. By beginning work showing appreciation to this state the therapist prepares it to become cooperative later in the process.

Using the Vivify Specific Action a second time, ask the patient to describe in detail a specific time immediately prior to the commencement of addictive behavior. Then, ask the patient to, within that imagery, postpone the addictive behavior temporarily. Postponing the addictive behavior will create angst in the Vaded State. The purpose of addictive behavior is to avoid the Vaded State coming into the Conscious, therefore when this behavior is postponed the Vaded State will begin to come into the Conscious.

When it is obvious that the Vaded State has assumed the Conscious (by observing the affect of the patient), Bridge and use Actions 4 to 7 to resolve the issue of the Vaded State.

Use the RT Action 10, Retro State Negotiation, to ensure that future emotionally challenging times will not result in the Retro State returning to retro behavior. RT Action 10 will ensure that the state has volunteered to conduct positive behavior in the future, if needed.

Finally, use RT Action 12, Check Imagery, in order to check the efficacy of the intervention, and to allow the patient to experience and practice using a positive Resource State within the imagery.

Depression

There are two kinds of depression, organically based depression and psychologically-based depression. Organically based depression can be caused by chemical imbalances, drug use, or physiology. Psychologically-based depression is caused by a profound level of disappointment in the perceived reality. Both types of depression result in physiological changes in the body. The presentation in this book relates to psychologically-based depression, and when the word depression is used it will refer to psychologically-based depression.

Depression is often misdiagnosed, with a number of patients presenting with the belief that they are depressed when they really have Resource States Vaded with Fear, Rejection, or Confusion. Resource States Vaded with Disappointment relate to depression.

The patient suffering from depression will be low in energy, and will have a state with such a profound level of disappointment that it will block other states in their ability to enjoy living. Often, the patient will know exactly why he or she is depressed, but sometimes the patient is unaware of the reason the disappointed Resource State is blocking other states.

The RT intervention for depression is somewhat similar to the CBT intervention. A CBT therapist will normally encourage the patient to begin interacting in life; begin walking, and begin taking on more activities. It is not unusual for the depressed patient to fail in their attempts to reengage in these activities. The reason for this is the Resource State Vaded with Disappointment will most often continue to block other states from enjoying life, because of its disappointment.

The RT intervention for depression also begins with assisting the patient to reengage in living. A difference in the techniques is that the RT therapist speaks directly with the Resource States that have enjoyed activities in the past to ensure that they are willing to take on these activities, and also speaks with the Resource State that is Vaded with Disappointment to gain its permission for these Resource States to begin re-engaging. Therefore, patients more easily and more quickly can begin re-engaging. This is very important.

The depressed patient will need time to re-energize before therapy can be completed. Therefore, the quicker Resource States can take on positive activities, the speedier therapy can continue.

No therapy can result in a patient who is clinically depressed walking out in the first session in a normal condition. It physiologically takes the body a number of weeks to reengage to a normal level of energy.

The steps and RT Actions for the treatment of States Vaded with Disappointment should be followed to assist patients in their process to return to a normal level of energy. It should be noted that patients who have already begun the use of antidepressants will necessarily respond slower to many RT Actions because the antidepressants can make it more difficult to access Resource States. These patients may still benefit greatly from RT Actions, although the speed of their improvement may be affected.

Antidepressants may completely block some Resource States. For example, occasionally a patient suffering from OCD will discover an antidepressant can eliminate OCD symptoms. When this occurs, the antidepressant is blocking from the conscious the Vaded State that is the root of OCD avoiding behavior. The Retro Avoiding State has no need to carry out OCD avoiding behavior when this Vaded State is being blocked chemically. Of course, it is better to resolve the issues of the Vaded State, when possible, without the use of chemical intervention.

I will sometimes tell patients that when they, and their doctors, decide that it is time to cut back or stop the use of antidepressants that I would like to see them if they begin experiencing emotional setbacks. As states that were chemically blocked begin to surface RT actions may be used to resolve their issues.

Antidepressants do not block all states. RT Actions may be used with any patient using antidepressants. Therapeutic intervention for some patients goes more slowly, while for other patients therapeutic intervention seems to not be affected by the use of antidepressants.

Fear of Engagement

Fear of engagement can be debilitating. It can keep people from entering into employment, relationships, and can even keep people from leaving the house. Patients suffering with fear of engagement are not in control of their own lives. They often fight their fear, and they often lose.

The patient who fears engaging with others, whether it has to do with work or social activities, most normally has a State Vaded with Rejection. Occasionally, this can be caused by a State Vaded with Fear. If patients report feelings of concern about how they will be seen by others then they have a fear of rejection.

The following statements will indicate a patient has a State Vaded with Rejection:

- I am afraid they will not like me.
- I am afraid of the way they will see me.
- I am too old.
- I am too fat.
- I would be too embarrassed.
- I am afraid my work will not be good enough.
- I might let the other person down.

The following statements will indicate the patient has a State Vaded with Fear:

- I don't like to leave the house at night.
- Sometimes I have feelings of panic.

- I just can't make myself get on the airplane.

- I feel overwhelmed when I think about going out.

Patients with fear of engagement normally have practiced attempting to push that fear away so they can continue with their lives in as normal a manner as possible. This is an understandable reaction, but a reaction that actually can exacerbate their problem.

The patient with a fear of engagement will have a vaded childhood state. A childhood Resource State is hanging onto the illusion that something internally may either hurt it or reject it. When this childhood Vaded State comes to the surface bringing with it its insecurities, the last thing it needs to experience is to be pushed away.

Imagine a little child afraid or upset, holding hands high, wanting to be rescued or wanting to be made safe. Imagine this little child being given the message by more mature states, "Leave me alone. Get out of here. I don't want you here." This is the experience of the Vaded State that attempts to come to the surface and is pushed away. The result is often that this state becomes more upset and those upset feelings may interfere even more with the life the patient.

When this state learns that it can be safe in its inner space, and when this state is connected with a Resource State that enjoys nurturance, it can feel safe and supported. Then, it will no longer interfere with the current life of the patient, and the patient's more mature Resource States can handle life's challenges.

Resource Therapy Actions 2, Vivify Specific, to Action 7, Relief, should be used to bring a Vaded State with Fear or Rejection to a condition of normality. These Actions will result in the childhood Vaded State gaining feelings of support.

Panic Disorder and PTSD

Panic Disorder and PTSD are caused by states Vaded with Fear. A Resource State has experienced something extremely scary, often interpreted as life-threatening, and then that Resource State has not received any appropriate crisis intervention following the event. When this occurs this Resource State will hang onto the negative feelings, will interpret them as still happening internally, and when that Resource State comes to the Conscious it will bring with it the same panic it experienced during the initial sensitizing event.

When bridging occurs, taking the patient back to the initial sensitizing event, the therapist is able to interact with the Vaded State as it felt at that time. It will be expressing the same feelings that it experiences during a panic attack. A panic attack during a therapy session is referred to as an abreaction. Patients who abreact during a session reveal that they are experiencing the unresolved emotions of a Resource State Vaded with Fear.

Unless the therapist is capable of working with a Resource State that is frightened and upset bridging should not be undertaken. If the therapist bridges a patient suffering from panic attack or PTSD to an initial sensitizing event and then immediately attempts to get the patient to relax and feel better, a re-traumatizing will have occurred. In other words taking a patient to a traumatic event and then backing out, and doing nothing, only brings the patient closer to those traumatized feelings. But, if the patient is taken to an initial sensitizing event and the Vaded State is helped to understand

- that the Introjects within that event no longer exist,

- that it is now safe,

- that it can say anything it wants to say safely, and

- that it can have additional safety and support from other stronger mature Resource States,

then de-traumatizing has occurred. The previously Vaded State is no longer Vaded, as it has returned to a Normal Condition, with feelings of safety and support. It can even return to its original role, whether that was play or something else. If it was play, the patient most often will report finding an additional ability to enjoy playful moments in life.

The one thing that is most important in ensuring that the State Vaded with Fear moves to a Normal Condition is to ensure that the Vaded State is in the Conscious during the intervention process. The Vaded State will not receive a resolution if the therapist is talking with an intellectual state. As soon as a name is received for the Vaded State it should continue to be called by that name and all questions should relate to its experiences and feelings. Intellectual questions such as, "Why," or "What do you think of this" should be avoided. Questions such as these take the patient away from the Vaded State and into an intellectual state.

When the state that has carried the fearful feelings is Conscious, and while Conscious if it receives the intervention (Actions 4 to 7), then it is no longer Vaded. It is in a normal condition.

The process of moving a State Vaded with Fear to a state of normality can happen very quickly. Afterwards, patients will show immediate change and this change is permanent. There is an obvious difference in the feelings of the state once RT Actions 4 through 7 have been completed.

Abuse

Most patients who have suffered abuse have Resource States Vaded with Fear. It is not unusual for them also to have Resource States Vaded with Rejection.

An important aspect about working with the patient who has suffered abuse is to refrain from assuming that the presented issue is directly associated with that abuse. Too often both patients and therapists assume that issues relate to abuse, even when they do not. Of course, many issues do relate to abuse, but the bridging techniques in RT Action 3, Bridging, will be able to locate the initial sensitizing event that relates to changes the patient is interested in making.

All patients have issues, not only patients who have suffered abuse. There is no need to revisit negative times in the lives of patients unless doing so results in resolving the issues that patients are ready to change.

When bridging takes a patient to an initial sensitizing event involving abuse the patient does not need to go into any detail about that abuse. Resolution has to do with empowerment. It does not have to do with regurgitating details. RT is not a voyeuristic therapy. What is important is that the state that sees the Introject of an abuser as powerful, learns that that Introject has no power within the personality. It is important for the Resource State that felt disempowered to learn that it can now have the space where it is in control, safe, supported and loved.

The patient does not have to go into any detail about anything that has happened. It is important for the state that was Vaded with Fear to be able to express fully to the abuser, and that state is better enabled to do this with the help of the therapist. The therapist can say things like, "Let's just shrink him down to 1 inch tall," or "Is it okay if I talk to him first?"

It is important for the state that was Vaded with Fear to be able to express fully to the abuser so that it can realize there is now nothing inside that can hurt it. It realizes this by experiencing that it can say absolutely anything completely freely. When it realizes this, then it has the power to ask the abuser to leave its inner space. Therefore, a Resource State that had been Vaded, can become empowered, can gain a feeling of safety, and with RT Action 7, Relief, it can feel supported and loved. It can be left in a bright, loving space, no longer hanging on to fears from the past.

This kind of intervention does not change the past, it changes what the person continues to carry from the past. Revisiting a negative memory will always be difficult, but when the patient no longer carries the seething emotions of fear and rejection from the past, that patient will be able to respond to current challenges with mature Resource States that can best deal with them.

The patient who presents with a State Vaded with Fear will be able to discover with the therapist if that state was Vaded during abuse or during any other time. See the section, Vaded with Fear, on page 61 for the precise steps to follow to work with Resource States Vaded with Fear.

Complicated Bereavement: Working with Grief and Loss

Beginnings and endings are special things. Births and deaths bring a reality to the meaning of life. People who have witnessed these often gain a greater appreciation for the time that is spent here.

There's a natural process in grieving, whether it is grieving the loss of a loved one, or grieving some other type of loss. Grieving can appropriately be a bittersweet experience, bitter because of the sadness and sweet because of the memory of the love. Sadness can be a reflection of love. The loving parent can feel sad when their child is hurt.

Patients who present in therapy with grieving as an issue may merely need education, or they may be suffering from a type of complicated bereavement. It is good to understand what is normal in grieving, and what is associated with complicated bereavement.

It is normal, when a person suffers loss, for that person to experience a deep sadness. This type of sadness is not a heavy, negative feeling. It is a reflection of the love or appreciation that was felt. It is normal to miss the person, or what was lost. It is normal to reflect in a wistful way. It is normal to cry. Some people cry without tears. It is normal to feel out of control in terms of when happiness may be felt or in terms of when tears may come. It is normal to continue to feel a connection, or a presence, and it is also normal not to. It is normal in the first few days of grieving to feel confusion, anger, regret, or blame.

These feelings of confusion, anger, regret, or blame are heavy feelings. They relate to something negative. Whereas sadness is, "Something I love is not here," heavier feelings connect with, "Someone did something wrong."

It is these heavier feelings that relate to complicated bereavement. If a patient presents having experienced these heavier feelings for an extended period of time a therapeutic intervention is important. There is no need for the natural process of grieving to be chronically interrupted by negative, heavy feelings. A Resource State Vaded with Confusion most often results with these feelings.

Patients who present with grieving as their issue will normally either have a Resource State Vaded with Confusion or a Resource State Vaded with Disappointment.

A Resource State Vaded with Disappointment is connected to depression and or blocking behavior. The person with the Resource State Vaded with Disappointment will exhibit a lower level of energy and will refuse to reengage in many aspects of living. If the patient exhibits these symptoms then the therapeutic procedures should be followed for a Resource State Vaded with Disappointment.

More common for a patient presenting with grief as an issue is a Resource Vaded with Confusion. This person will be able to participate normally in many aspects of living, but will be unable to let go of a deep level of confusion surrounding their loss. While patients should not be encouraged to "let go" of something loved, patients should also not have to experience a negative rumination surrounding the loss.

A patient with a Resource State Vaded with Confusion will report, "I just can't stop thinking about it." They will report things like, "I just wish I had said..., I just can't understand why..., or, I just can't get over this anger."

The process of assisting someone to let go of rumination is not the same thing as assisting someone to let go of the love or appreciation that was felt.

By letting go of negative and heavy emotions, patients will be able to better connect with the love and appreciation that they have.

In order to assist a patient in letting go of the confusion around a loss, straightforward RT Actions can be used for working with Resource States Vaded with Confusion. The core action in helping the patient let go of confusion is the Changing Chairs Introject Action.

It will be important for the patient working with grief to speak with the Introject that any negative feelings relate to. For example, the patient may speak with the Introject of their deceased loved one, express to that person any feelings and regrets that are held, then change to the chair of the deceased loved one. While in the chair of the deceased loved one the patient will have an opportunity to respond from that Introject. Then, when returning to their own chair their level of confusion will have changed.

The feelings that are experienced in the chair of the Introject are brought back to the patient, and this can provide a cathartic experience of relief and understanding. It is interesting that talking directly with a patient for weeks cannot bring the same emotional relief as the Changing Chairs Introject Action provides in one session.

When working with grief, patients may be asked to speak to the Introject of a pet, of God, to a person with whom they are angry, or to any other Introject that is involved in the negative feelings. It is important for them, when in the Introject's chair, to be encouraged to speak as if they are the Introject, as a great actor would. In other words, it is important for them to emotionally respond as the Introject.

This RT Action can result in the letting go of confusion, while, when desired, maintaining a loving connection.

It is always important to relate empathetically with patients who present with grieving as an issue. They will vary greatly in regards to their level of grief, and in regards to what they have lost. A patient may have lost a loved one, a pet, their health, a relationship, their youth, or any of a large number of other things that they have appreciated. The common factor in grieving is that there was something of importance that has been lost.

Eating Disorders (Anorexia and Bulimia)

The eating disorders of anorexia and bulimia are very different, but they are both caused by States Vaded with Rejection.

The patient suffering from anorexia has felt unable to gain a close, unconditional relationship with a parent or Guardian. This does not mean that that relationship was not offered, but it does mean that a relationship of unconditional love was not experienced. The patient suffering from anorexia has felt a deep yearning for connection, and has often developed perfectionistic traits in an attempt to gain approval, and thereby connection.

When it is discovered that a connection can be found by losing weight, a profound subconscious dynamic is created. The person who has found it impossible to feel a close unconditionally caring connection finally finds expressions of real concern as the body becomes thinner.

This dynamic is unplanned and subconscious, but difficult to break. The anorexic patient may find creative ways to lose weight, including starving, laxatives, bulimic behavior, and exercise. All of these behaviors are Retro Avoiding, avoiding the experience of the Vaded State that yearns for connection.

One reason this dynamic is difficult to break is the often absence of a nurturing state in the anorexic patient. The anorexic patient has experienced such a profound and chronic desire for nurturance that this person has often not developed an unconditionally loving nurturing part. Therefore, the RT Action 7, Relief, becomes difficult.

The anorexic patient has a Vaded State in great need of nurturance, and has often not developed a nurturing state that can offer that internally. Over a number of sessions a Resource State that can take on the role of nurturance can develop its skills and offer more and more internal acceptance and appreciation.

The Find Resource Action can be used to locate the state that has the best potential of developing a higher level of nurturing ability. This state can be negotiated with directly so it can practice nurturance and become better at nurturing the State Vaded with Rejection.

Work with anorexic patients often takes a number of weeks before the state that needs acceptance can gain it internally.

Bulimia is used in an attempt to lose weight, or not gain it. While the anorexic patient may use bulimia to lose weight, many patients use bulimia to compete with others, who they see as more appealing than themselves. These patients suffer from low self-esteem due to having a Vaded State with Rejection. They feel, "I am not good enough," and in order to be good enough they will go to great lengths. Like anorexia, bulimia is harmful physiologically.

When bulimia is not associated with anorexia it is easier to treat. Patients may respond quickly when the associated Vaded State is brought into the Conscious, Bridged, and resolved.

With both anorexia and bulimia it is important that the associated Vaded State be brought into the Conscious prior to the direct work with the Retro Avoiding State that is responsible for the unwanted behavior. This can be done easily with the imagery of withholding the problematic behavior, which results in the angst of the Vaded State surfacing. These are the same techniques that are used with any Retro Avoiding Behavior.

Rage issues

The patient who has rage as an issue has a Retro Original Resource State. The rage Resource State has almost always developed in childhood. It is important to always talk positively to and about all Resources, and the rage Resource State is no exception. The rage state may have carried out activities that were inappropriate, or even illegal. Still, the patient has come to therapy for change and the best way to effect change is to connect positively with all Resource States.

The rage Resource State can be told that it is good for the person to have such a strong state, that every person could benefit from such a state, and that it is also good to be liked and appreciated by the other parts of the personality. All states like to be liked, even those who say that they don't care.

The key to helping the patient who presents with rage is to connect in a positive way to the state that exhibits rage, to find an alternative Resource that can be assertive, and make sure that the patient has the ability to determine which state should be conscious at the appropriate time.

The core RT Action that is involved in this process is Retro State Negotiation. The rage state has not felt appreciated in the past. It can be told that it should be appreciated, and that it can be appreciated by all states. It will often at first not believe this.

A suggestion can be made that it is such a powerful state that it only need come out to protect the body from physical danger. A suggestion can be made that during other times it would be more appropriate for an assertive state to come out. This gives the rage state an important role, and in most people's lives the state will never again assume the consciousness.

The rage state may be accessed using the Vivify Specific Action, and an assertive state may be accessed using the Find Resource Action. When a patient presents with rage as an issue I often first locate a state that can take on assertive behavior prior to speaking with the Resource that takes on rage behavior. That way, when talking with a rage state I can refer to the assertive state with confidence that it will understand what I'm talking about. Here are the steps for working with rage:

- Use RT Action 8, to find a Resource that can be Assertive.

- Use RT Action 2, to bring into the Conscious the Resource that sometimes Rages.

- Show appreciation to the Rage Resource and suggest that it only come out when the body is physically in danger, and that at other times the Assertive state can handle the smaller things.

- Speak with the Resource State that brought the patient to therapy and suggest how it would be positive if the rage Resource were available to protect the body when it was in danger, and if the assertive Resource were available to respond to other challenging issues.

- Make sure that this Resource responds directly to the rage Resource, saying that it would appreciate it if it would protect the body from danger, and allow the assertive Resource to respond at other times.

- Speak again with the rage Resource saying something like, "Did you hear that? You will be liked and appreciated by the other states if you are there to do the very important role of protecting the body. They will all like you and pat you on the back. It is appropriate that they appreciate you because you are an important part of this person."

- Negotiate with the rage Resource and the assertive Resource making sure that both are pleased with the outcome.

- Use the Find Resource Action to locate a wise state that can decide which Resource is the best Resource at any given time. Make sure this Resource speaks directly with both the rage Resource and the assertive Resource.

- Use RT Action 12, Imagery Check, to ensure that all Resources understand their agreements.

Following these actions all resources have defined roles, all resources are appreciated, and a wise Resource is left with a responsibility to decide when it is appropriate to be assertive and when it might be appropriate to defend against a pack of wild dogs.

Chapter 6: The Art of applying Resource Therapy

This section offers a discussion about techniques for obtaining the best results with Resource Therapy. Metaphorically, if Resource Therapy is thought of as the archer's bow, the tool, then this section has to do with the focus and mindset of the archer.

The Bow

Resource Therapy is an amazing tool. It is common for a therapist to comment to me after using the therapy for the first time following a workshop, with something like, "I saw a patient that I had been working with for 6 years and I decided to use some of these techniques. My patient said it was the best session we had ever had. There was more movement in that session than we had ever had."

The Focus and Mindset

We should love our profession. Therapy is a profession that should not be entered into solely to make money. For the better therapists, it will always be a passion. It is an honor to be trusted enough to be a person who is told one's deepest secrets. I feel lucky that people come to me and trust me and share with me. I feel honored, and I want to respect that trust.

The therapist patient relationship is important and needs to be honored and preserved. Patients come to see therapists often in a very fragile condition, often with unclear boundaries, and sometimes having had abusive relationships. It is important for them to feel a rock-solid therapeutic relationship with the person they have sought for help.

I attempt to avoid saying anything that could blur the patient therapist boundary line. For example, I would not say to a patient, "You look nice today." A statement like that sounds innocuous, but could be interpreted as, "He is noticing something personal about me, about how I physically look." It is better to maintain a focus on what needs to be done in therapy and avoid any personal statements that could fog the therapist patient boundaries.

This is especially important when using Resource Therapy. Resource Therapy often requires patients to revisit initial sensitizing events where they felt disrespected, abused, or frightened. Therefore, the patient's experience of very clear and honored boundaries with the therapist is highly important.

If at any point in therapy the therapeutic boundary seems to be challenged or misunderstood by the patient, a good way of handling that misunderstanding is to generally review an initial therapeutic information sheet. Say something like, "I see this is our fourth session today. I always like to review the therapeutic information sheet on the fourth session, just to make sure there are no questions." As part of the general review I include things like confidentiality and therapeutic boundaries, where there is a clear and distinct boundary between the therapist and the patient and in no way can that boundary be crossed. I find by covering this in a 'matter of fact' manner a misunderstanding in boundaries can be put to rest without embarrassing the patient.

There is a lot to learn in this primer, and more to learn in the main text. It can take a while to learn the RT Actions and how to quickly diagnose Resource States. It is expected that while learning, the therapist will have to review either notes or mental files within a session. Still, outside those times where the therapist must think about the next step, the primary focus needs to be inside the story of the patient.

I like to think about where the focus is in the therapy room. For example, if my mind were to wonder to what I would be doing after the therapy session, obviously, my focus would not even be in the room, and I would not be doing good therapy. If my focus is thinking about whether I am a good therapist, a poor therapist, doing well, or doing poorly then my focus is on myself rather than inside story of the patient.

The best therapists will allow their point of focus to be inside the patient. Everything else about self, the room, anything outside the room, needs to be left behind. The singular focus needs to be inside the story of the patient. It is when that focus stays with the patient that creative therapy follows.

Not only does the focus need to be inside the story of the patient, it needs to be focused on the affect of the patient. It is emotional issues that bring patients to therapy.

A person can think really crazy thoughts and as long as they are emotionally peaceful they will not seek therapy. We probably all know some neighbors, friends, or family members that fall into that category.

It is only when a person feels emotionally distressed that they will decide to seek therapy. Therapy is about helping patients feel better. Patients may be upset about the feelings they are having, upset about the behaviors they are doing, upset about inner conflict, or about their performance. The bottom line is, patients come to therapy because they are upset, not because of how they think.

It is useful to imagine a line at the neck that divides thinking from feeling. Patients may make above the neck statements or they may relate below the neck experiences or feelings. When we are working with Resource States, because patients issues are about feelings, it is almost always necessary to focus on states that are speaking from below the neck.

Because it is so important to speak with the correct Resource State, the Resource State that has the issue, it is important to avoid bringing out an intellectual Resource State. When therapists are training they will often say to their patients things like, "Why do you do that?" This is an 'above the neck' question. The result of this question will be to bring an intellectual Resource State into the Conscious. A question like this slows therapy. If RT Action 2, Vivify Specific, has been used to bring the desired Resource State to the Conscious, a 'why' question will force that state out of the Conscious so an intellectual state can think about it, and come up with an answer.

Intellectual states are great resources. They help us do our taxes, they help us with math, they can help us consider major decisions, and they can help us plan. Intellectual resources are good states to have in the Conscious when we are hearing criticism. They can, without emotion, make decisions regarding the relevance of criticism. They are great personality parts, but they are also great places to escape.

The intellect is a barren wasteland in terms of emotion. It is good to have a computer on our desktop or in our head, but it is not a computer that defines us. We connect with others and with ourselves emotionally. We like our friends to be open with their feelings, and we feel understood when others show that they hear our feelings. When we reflect about a sunset, about what we like, or about how we are doing, we are reflecting emotionally. It is our emotions that define us to others and to ourselves. It is emotions that bring patients to therapy, and it is emotions that need to be heard by therapists.

Vaded States are emotional states. By bridging from a State Vaded with Fear or Rejection we are taking the patient to an initial sensitizing event where emotions are unsettled. Especially, during this process it is important to speak with the client about feelings and experiences. Any reference to interpretation or thinking will necessarily remove the emotional Vaded State from the Conscious so that an intellectual consideration can be made by an intellectual state.

When patients relate experiences or feelings they are connecting with emotions. They are connecting with Resource States that are not above the neck. These are the states that need the brought to the Conscious, and held in the Conscious until a resolution is found. The art of therapy, and especially the art of Resource Therapy entails being able to maintain a conversation with the Resource States that need change. It is good to be profoundly aware that focusing in a safe and respectful way where emotions are held is a wellspring of therapeutic change.

Supervision

This section relates to some of the issues brought up during supervision sessions with Resource Therapists. I supervise a number of therapists who have studied Resource Therapy. There are some common issues they bring to supervision that may be beneficial to address here.

Bridging

Therapist: "I am having trouble bridging. I'm not sure I'm getting to the initial sensitizing event."

Supervisor: "Tell me exactly what you say during the bridging process. What exactly do you say to the patient?"

Therapist: "I tell them to go to the first time they remember having this feeling."

Supervisor: "When you use the word remember, you are asking the patient to intellectually remember something. That is taking the patient away from their Vaded State, into an intellectual state. The only way they will be able to bridge is by having their Vaded State in the Conscious. It is the feelings of the Vaded State that allows that state to connect with the event that caused those feelings. Make sure, while you are bridging, that you only ask about experiences and feelings. Never ask the patient to remember, think back, or think about when was the first time you experienced this? It is impossible to bridge unless the patient is in the Vaded State."

Therapist: "When should I bridge?"

Supervisor: "You should bridge when the patient has a State Vaded with Fear or Rejection. There are other techniques for helping patients with the other types of pathological Resource States."

Changing Chairs Introject Action

Therapist: "I wanted to use the Changing Chairs Introject Action, and my patient was not comfortable with that. She felt silly talking to an empty chair."

Supervisor: "How did you introduce that Action to her?"

Therapist: "I told her there was an activity I would like to try. I asked her if she would be comfortable talking to an empty chair, pretending that her husband was there?"

Supervisor: "You are the professional therapist. The patient has come to you for your professional understanding of techniques, and for you to select the techniques that will help her get to get the change that she desires. It will be easier for the patient when you tell her clearly the steps you want her to follow. If a person goes to a medical doctor with a wound filled with dirt the doctor will not ask the patient if the patient thinks that wound should be cleaned out and scrubbed, or left the way it is. The medical doctor knows that the wound should be cleaned and gives the patient clear instructions so that the wound can be cleaned. In the same way, if you see that the Changing Chairs Introject Activity will help your patient become less confused, it is better not to put the responsibility of which technique to use on to the patient. Merely pull an empty chair in front of the patient, and clearly say, 'This is what I want you to do.' The patient will follow your clear instructions, will not be stressed about having to make a therapeutic decision, and will benefit from your professional knowledge."

Holding a State in the Conscious

Therapist: "I am having trouble holding the emotional state in the Conscious. I can get the state into the conscious using the Vivify Specific Action, but then it seems like another state takes over."

Supervisor: "As soon as you get a Resource State into the Conscious it is important to get a name for it, and continue to call it by that name. If you use its name constantly, almost in every sentence, it will stay in the conscious. It is also helpful to think about talking directly to that state. When states are addressed directly they continue to stay in the Conscious. An example is, if someone sees you may be a bit emotional and if they make a statement recognizing your emotions, that will bring that emotional state into the Conscious. It has been spoken to."

Therapist: "What is the best way to ask a Resource State to name itself."

Supervisor: "It is better not to say, 'What can I call this part of you?' When you recognize the state that you want to speak with is in the Conscious, say, 'What can I call you, the part that (e.g., is feeling upset)'. Imagine being in a room full of people and wanting to know the person's name you are speaking with. You would not say to that person, 'What can I call this person I'm talking with?' You would say, 'What can I call you? It is always important to speak directly to a Resource State as if you are talking to an individual. That will help it stay in the Conscious, and that will help it feel respected."

Vivify Specific

Therapist: "I'm not sure I'm getting the right Resource State into the Conscious in order to do therapeutic work. The Vivify Specific Action does not seem to be working for me."

Supervisor: "Tell me exactly what you are saying to the patient."

Therapist: "I tell him to tell me about a time he felt upset."

Supervisor: "That sounds good. Then what happens?"

Therapist: "He tells me he feels upset most at work. But it seems like he stays in an intellectual Resource State."

Supervisor: "Are you making sure he tells you about one specific instance when he felt upset at work?"

Therapist: "Probably not. He just tells me he feels upset at work."

Supervisor: "That is an intellectual state telling about the problem. That is not the state that actually experiences the problem. In order to gain access to the state that actually experiences the problem you have to get him to tell you about a specific instance, and then have him to tell more about that instance in detail, while you speak with him in the present tense."

Therapist: "What do you mean the present tense?"

Supervisor: "It is not the present tense if you say to him, 'What was the expression on your boss's face?' It is the present tense if you say to him, 'Right now, sitting at your desk, in the middle of the afternoon, what is your boss looking like, as he is looking at you?' In order to Vivify Specific, you must first have the patient describe in detail one specific incident, and you must begin to talk with the patient about being inside that incident using present tense. It is much easier to do this when you ask patients to allow their eyes to close, immediately prior to the Vivify Specific Action. Patients are better able to connect with an event with their eyes closed, because they are not having to process all the visual information in front of them."

Therapist: "When do I know they are in the right Resource State?"

Supervisor: "You will be able to recognize that. There's a big difference between talking with an intellectual state about something, and with talking to the state that is emotional. It is clear when a nervous Resource State comes into the Conscious."

Duck Billed Platypus Therapy

Therapist: "Sometimes it seems like this just isn't going to go anywhere. I get lost and I don't know what to do next."

Supervisor: "Yes, that happens to me to. I practice what I called the Duck Billed Platypus form of therapy."

Therapist: "What's that?"

Supervisor: "A Duck Billed Platypus swims underwater with his eyes closed. When it bumps into a rock it backs up, moves over to the side, and goes forward again. If it bumps into the rock a second time, it backs up moves over again, and goes forward. It continues to do this until he gets around the rock. If I try something in therapy and it doesn't work, I remember what the patient is ready to change, I back up a bit, move over, and try something else. That does not mean I will get around every rock, but it does help me in working with patients."

Highly emotional patients

Therapist: "When I bridged my patient became so emotional she said she did not want to continue."

99

Supervisor: "It is understandable that patients will become emotional. That is often why they are coming to therapy. When we work with the patient to bridge to an emotional initial sensitizing event, it is especially understandable that they may feel unable to handle the situation. That is why it is still something that is bothering them currently. Because we know it is only an illusion, an Introject from the past, that is problematic for them we can show strength and understanding. This will help them become empowered. If, after bridging, the patient says to me, 'I can't do this,' I will say something like, 'That's OK. We don't have to. Since we know this isn't happening now, if you could do this, what kind of thing would you have liked to have said?' Another thing I might say is, 'That's fine. We don't have to. Let's just shrink him down to 1 inch tall. He is tiny with a squeaky little voice. Please don't step on him, because I want you to be able to tell him what you want to say.' The key is to help the patient feel comfortable. Do not say that we have to continue. Tell the patient it is fine not to continue, but then help the patient understand that all the power is held by the Resource State. It is much better to leave a Resource State feeling empowered, expressed, understood, protected, and cared for, than to back out and leave the Resource State holding the same fear that it has felt for years."

Introducing Resource Therapy to Patients

Therapist: "How do I introduce Resource Therapy to my patients?"

Supervisor: "When I have a new patient, I merely say that the personality is composed of parts; part of me might want to do one thing while another part might like to do something else. I say that I work to make sure that I speak directly with the part that needs change. Then I ask if there are any questions. Actually, very few patients have questions following this introduction, but if they do I answer them."

Glossary

Changing Chairs Introject Action: This is a resource activity designed to assist patients to hold less confusion in relation to an Introject. The patient is instructed to imagine the essence of an Introject in an empty chair, to say everything that they would like to say to that Introject, then to move into that chair and speak as the Introject back to the patient, expressing how what was just said made the Introject feel. It often results in a cathartic sense of understanding.

Conscious: The Conscious is held by the Resource State that is currently aware and behaving. When a different Resource State takes over the Conscious, sense of self, emotions, behavior and abilities, change. The Conscious awareness may change from intellectual and reflective to reactive and emotional with a change of Resource State.

Conflicted States: Resources in a conflicted condition are in a level of conflict with another Resource to the extent that the individual experiences psychological distress. While it is common and appropriate that Resources hold different opinions (I would really like the car, and there's no way I can afford a new car)Conflicted States achieve a level of conflict that becomes stressful to the patient.

Dissonant States: A Resource State that is in the Conscious at the wrong time.

Resource (State): A personality part that was created by the repetition of returning over and over again to a coping skill. It is a physiological part of the nervous system created by axon and dendrite growth and trained synaptic firings. Each Resource manifests the traits of the coping skills that formed it. Each will have its own level of emotion, intellect, and abilities. Whenever a person is Conscious there is a Resource holding the Conscious.

Resource Personality Theory: A theory that assumes that personality is composed of separate parts, called Resources. Resource therapists assume that the most direct way to promote change is to work specifically with the Resource that is troubled, rather than with an intellectual state that can easily talk about the problem.

Imagery Check: At the beginning of the intervention the Vivify Specific Action is used to locate the Resource that requires change. Following the intervention, the Imagery Check is used to return to this initial image to test the effectiveness of the intervention, to give the patient practice in a similar setting in the future, and to give the patient confidence that the intervention has been effective. If the Imagery Check reveals no change, there is an indication that more therapeutic work is required relating to the issue.

Intellectual Memory: An Intellectual Memory is one that when recalling an occurrence the emotional experience is not relived. Intellectual memories may be held by states that did not experience the original event. Sensory Experience Memories differ from Intellectual memories in that the recalling process includes the emotional experience of the original event.

Intellectual Protector States: These are protector states that come to the Conscious to protect the personality from the emotional feelings of Vaded States. During therapy Intellectual Protector States may attempt to block the therapist from Bridging to the Vaded State that needs resolution. The patient intellectualizes, rather than feels. The Intellectual Protector State normally dislikes the Vaded State, seeing it as a state that gets in the way.

Initial Sensitising Event: This is a difficult and emotional event that has overwhelmed a Normal Resource, causing it to become a Vaded State. Later, when this Vaded State comes to the Conscious it brings with it the same negative emotional feelings that it experienced during the initial sensitizing event.

Introject: A Resource's internalized impression of another person, an animal, or an inanimate. Most Introjects are experienced as emotionally positive, but Vaded States hold Introjects from which they have experienced negative emotion. Introjects have only the power given them by the Resource States that hold them.

Normal States: Resources in the Normal condition exhibit psychological health. They function well both externally and within the personality. They are not conflicted with other states and they do not hold psychological distress.

Protector States: Therapeutic resistance is caused by protector states. These are states that attempt to protect fragile Vaded States from coming to the Conscious where the personality would experience the overwhelming emotions they feel. Behavioral examples of protector states coming into the Conscious include anger, withdrawal, intellectualizing, and perseveration. Protector States merely deflect attention, while Retro Avoiding States conduct unwanted behavior to save the personality from the negative feelings of Vaded States.

Retro Avoiding States: Retro States that learn to hold the Conscious to avoid the experience of a Vaded State. In problem gambling, the state that gambles is a Retro Avoiding State. It has learned to protect the patient from a painful Vaded emotion filled state by filling the Consciousness with gambling activity. Other Resources will dislike this gambling Resource, but the Retro State believes its role in saving the patient from the negative emotions of the Vaded State is more important than the disapproval it endures. Other examples of Retro Avoiding States include the states that cause a patient to feel numb, states that act out OCD behavior, self-harming states, and states that are involved with eating disorder activities. These states will hold a strong compulsion to maintain their "helping" behavior as long as the emotional state they protect the patient from remains vaded.

Retro Original States: These are states that have learned a functional coping skill in childhood that is no longer wanted by the patient. Much antisocial behavior is a result of Retro Original States and examples include passive aggressive behavior and rage. These Retro States will continue to see their role as important, until they can be negotiated with to take on an altered or lesser role.

Retro States: Resources that, when conscious, act in ways that other Resources (and usually other people) find problematic. There are two types of Retro States, Retro Original States and Retro Avoiding States. Antisocial behavior, gambling, OCD behavior, and Eating Disorder behavior are examples of Retro States assuming the Conscious.

Sensory Experience Memory: A Sensory Experience Memory is one that, when experienced, the person emotionally re-experiences the original event. A Sensory Experience Memory is most normally experienced only closer in time to the event. For example, immediately after experiencing something emotional, good or bad, it is common to relive the emotional experience during recall. As time passes, most Sensory Experience Memories are transformed into Intellectual Memories. Sensory Experience Memories may only be experienced in the longer term when the Resource State that had the original experience is holding the Conscious.

States Vaded with Confusion: Following an initial sensitizing event, this Resource is left with a fundamental and profound level of confusion, and its response to this lack of ability to understand is a profoundly uncomfortable unknowing. While Resources Vaded with Fear, Rejection, or Disappointment hold a distinctly negative emotion, Resources Vaded with Confusion exhibit anxiety about what is not known to a level that is problematic to the patient. These states are often characterised by rumination.

States Vaded with Disappointment: This Resource takes on an overwhelming feeling of disappointment because of the gulf between what was desired or expected in life and the perceived reality. It is not the magnitude of what has happened that vades this Resource, it is the interpretation of what has happened that vades the state. These states cause psychological depression.

States Vaded with Fear: Resources Vaded with Fear are carrying internal fear everywhere they go and when they come to the Conscious they bring it to the surface with them. Resources Vaded with Fear prevent patients from feeling free to live their lives in a way that they choose, and they are the root of many psychological disturbances.

States Vaded with Rejection: Resources Vaded with Rejection feel unlovable. This feeling of not being good enough drives the patient, when it comes to the Conscious, to experience emotions of disempowerment, and they sometimes create a need to be perfect, as expressed in over competitiveness, out-of-control purchasing, and eating disorders.

Surface Resources: Surface Resources, as opposed to Underlying Resources, are those that are used frequently. They normally share memories together, and often observe other surface states when one is in the Conscious. A Resource that is out at work, and a Resource that is out while travelling are examples of Surface States.

Underlying Resources: Underlying Resources, as opposed to Surface Resources, are those that have been out frequently in the past but currently seldom come into the Conscious. Most childhood states are underlying Resources, with memories not readily available to surface states. Vaded States are most commonly underlying states, which occasionally come to the Conscious harbouring feelings of angst.

Vaded Avoided States: Vaded States are problematic for a patient in two ways, they can be Vaded Conscious States or Vaded Avoided States. Vaded Avoided States do not hold the Conscious, but when they come near or temporarily into the Conscious a 'helping state' (a Retro Avoiding State) uses an addictive behavior to force the Vaded State out of the Conscious, saving the patient from having to re-experience the overwhelmingly bad feelings of the Vaded State.

Vaded Conscious States: Vaded States are problematic for a patient in two ways; they can be Vaded Conscious States or Vaded Avoided States. Vaded Conscious States come into and hold the Conscious, causing the patient to feel emotional and out-of-control while they do. When they come to the surface they bring with them their overwhelming negative emotions, and this is what the patient experiences when they are in the Conscious.

Vaded States: Resources that were in a Normal Condition prior to experiencing an initial sensitising event that, because there was no form of crisis intervention, left them feeling chronically overwhelmed with the negative emotions. These Resources, while in a Vaded condition, are the cause of much pathology.

Vivify Specific: This refers to vivifying a specific instance when a Resource has been in the Conscious in order to bring it back into the Conscious during therapy for the purpose of intervention. Some patients attempt to give the therapist general times a Resource has been out, and this presentation will not bring the desired Resource into the Conscious. The Vivify Specific Action requires very specific detail relating to a time the state has been conscious. During this process present tense language is used.

References

Berne, E. (1957). Ego states in Psychotherapy. American Journal of Psychotherapy, 11, 293 -309. Transactional analysis in psychotherapy: A systematic individual and social psychiatry. New York: Grove Press.

Blakemore, C., and Price, D. J. (1987), "The organization and post-natal development of area 18 of the cat's visual cortex", Journal of Physiology, 384, pp. 293–309.

Boswell, Louis K. (1987). The initial sensitizing event of emotional disorders. Medical Hypnoanalysis Journal, 2(4), Dec, pp. 155-160.

Bryck, Richard L.; Fisher, Philip A. (2011). Training the brain: Practical applications of neural plasticity from the intersection of cognitive neuroscience, developmental psychology, and prevention science. American Psychologist, Jul 25.

Buisseret, Pierre, Gary-Bobo, Elyane, and Imbert, Michel (1982)."Plasticity in the kitten's visual cortex: Effects of the suppression of visual experience upon the orientational properties of visual cortical cells", Developmental Brain Research, 4 (4), pp. 417–26.

de Graaf, Theo K., & van der Molen, Gjalt M. (1996). A Personal Sensitization Factor (PSF) mediating between life events and post-traumatic psychiatric or psychosomatic disease in adult life. The European Journal of Psychiatry, 10:3, Jul-Sep. 137-148.

Emmerson, G. J. (1999). What lies within: Ego states and other internal personifications. Australian Journal of Clinical Hypnotherapy & Hypnosis, 20(1), pp. 13-22.

Emmerson, G. J. (2003, 2007, 2010). Ego state therapy. Carmarthen, Wales: Crown House Publishing

Emmerson, G. J. (2006). Advanced skills and interventions in therapeutic counseling. Carmarthen, Wales: Crown House Publishing

Emmerson, G. J. (2011). Ego state personality theory. Australian Journal of Clinical Hypnotherapy and Hypnosis, 33(2), pp. 5-23.

Emmerson, G. J. (2012). Healthy Parts Happy Self. Charleston, SC, CreateSpace.

Emmerson, G. J. (2013). Ego State Conditions. Australian Journal of Clinical Hypnotherapy and Hypnosis, 35(1), 2013. pp. 5-27.

Emmerson, G. J. (2014). Resource Therapy. Blackwood Victoria, Australia: Old Golden Point Press.

Federn, P. (1953). Ego psychology and the psychosis. London: Image Publishers.

Guntrip, H. (1961). Personality structure and human interaction. London: Hogarth.

Holopainen, Debbi; Emmerson, Gordon J. (2002). Ego state therapy and the treatment of depression. Australian Journal of Clinical Hypnotherapy & Hypnosis, Vol 23(2), pp. 89-99.

Jacobson, E. (1964). The self and the object world. New York: International University Press.

Kernberg, O. (1976). Object relations theory and clinical psychoanalysis. New York: JasoncAronson.

Levin, Berry. (2010). Interaction of perinatal and pre-pubertal factors with genetic predisposition in the development of neural pathways involved in the regulation of energy homeostasis. Brain Research, Sep2010, Vol. 1350, p. 10-17

Mackey, Edward F. (2009). Age regression: A case study. Annals of the American Psychotherapy Assn. 12(4), Winter, 46-49.

Muir, Darwin W., Dalhousie, U., and Mitchell, Donald E. (1973), "Visual resolution and experience: Acuity deficits in cats following early selective visual deprivation", Science. 180 (4084), pp. 420–2.

Opperman, M. C., (2007). The creation and manifestation of reality through the re-enactment of subconscious conclusions and decisions. Dissertation Abstracts International: Section B: The Sciences and Engineering, 68:5-B, 3406.

Ritzman, Thomas A., (1992). Importance of identifying the initial sensitizing event. Medical Hypnoanalysis Journal, 7(3), Sep. pp. 98-104.

Schrott, L. M. (1997), "Effect of training and environment on brain morphology and behavior", ActaPaediatrica, 422, pp. 45–7.

Wark, Robert C., and Peck, Carol K. (1982), "Behavioral consequences of early visual exposure to contours of a single orientation", Developmental Brain Research, 5 (2), pp. 218–21.

Watkins, J. G. (1978). The therapeutic self. New York: Human Sciences.

Watkins, J. G. & Watkins, H. H. (1997). Ego states: Theory and therapy. New York: W. W. Norton& Co.

Wilkinson, Frances, and McGill, U. (1995), "Orientation, density and size as cues to texture segmentation in kittens", Vision Research, 35 (17), pp. 2463–78.

Winnicott, D. W. (1965). The maturational process and the facilitation environment. New York: International Universities Press.

Weiss, E. (1950). Principles of psychodynamics. New York: Grune& Stratton.

About the author

Dr Gordon Emmerson is an Honorary Fellow in the School of Psychology at Victoria University, Melbourne. He is the author of the books 'Ego State Therapy' (2003, 2007, 2010), 'Advanced Techniques in Therapeutic Counseling (2006), Healthy Parts Happy Self (2012), and Resource Therapy (2014). He developed Resource Personality Theory and Therapy and has developed techniques for working with many psychological conditions. As a registered psychologist and member of the Australian Psychological Society, he has published numerous refereed articles and has conducted and published experimental clinical research . Dr Emmerson has conducted workshops in Australia, South Africa, Germany, the UK, New Zealand, the US, and the Middle East. He makes keynote conference and convention addresses on his therapeutic approaches. He provides Foundation Training, a Clinical Qualification in Resource Therapy, Advanced Clinical Training in Resource Therapy, and Train the Trainer.

Upcoming workshops can be found on http://www.resourcetherapy.com.

Gordon Emmerson

www.ingramcontent.com/pod-product-compliance
Lightning Source LLC
Chambersburg PA
CBHW031215270326
41931CB00006B/570